STAGING ASYLUM, AGAIN

*Edited by Tania Canas
and Caroline Wake*

CURRENCY PRESS
The performing arts publisher

First published in 2023
by Currency Press
Gadigal Land, Suite 310, 46-56 Kippax Street, Surry Hlls NSW 2010, Australia
enquiries@currency.com.au
www.currency.com.au

This revised edition first published in 2024.

Introduction: Staging Asylum, Again and individual play introductions, copyright © Tania Cañas and Caroline Wake 2023; *Tribunal* copyright © PYT Fairfield 2023; *Going for Gold* copyright © Noëlle Janaczewska 2023; *Three Angry Australians* copyright © Tania Cañas; *A Puppet Show for All Ages* copyright © Georgia Symons 2023; *We All Know What's Happening* copyright © Samara Hersch and Lara Thoms, 2023; *The Audition* copyright © Patricia Cornelius, Tes Lyssiotis, Sahra Davoudi, Christos Tsiolkas, Melissa Reeves, Milad Norouzi, Wahibe Moussa and Outer Urban Projects, 2023.

COPYING FOR EDUCATIONAL PURPOSES
The Australian *Copyright Act* 1968 (Act) allows a maximum of one chapter or 10% of this book, whichever is the greater, to be copied by any educational institution for its educational purposes provided that that educational institution (or the body that administers it) has given a remuneration notice to Copyright Agency (CA) under the Act. For details of the CA licence for educational institutions contact CA, 12 / 66 Goulburn Street, Sydney, NSW, 2000; tel: within Australia 1800 066 844 toll free; outside Australia 61 2 9394 7600; fax: 61 2 9394 7601; email: memberservices@copyright.com.au.

COPYING FOR OTHER PURPOSES
Except as permitted under the Act, for example a fair dealing for the purposes of study, research, criticism or review, no part of this book may be reproduced, stored in a retrieval system, or transmitted in any form or by any means without prior written permission. All enquiries should be made to the publisher at the address above.

Any performance or public reading from *Staging Asylum, Again* is forbidden unless a licence has been received from the authors or the authors' agents. The purchase of this book in no way gives the purchaser the right to perform the plays in public, whether by means of a staged production or a reading. All applications for public performance should be addressed to the authors, c/– Currency Press.

Currency Press has made every reasonable effort to identify, and gain the permission of, the artists who appear in the photographs that illustrate these plays.

Typeset by Brighton Gray for Currency Press.
Cover design by Katherine Zhang for Currency Press. Cover art by Khalid Shatta.

Currency Press acknowledges the Traditional Owners of the Country on which we live and work. We pay our respects to all Aboriginal and Torres Strait Islander Elders, past and present.

A catalogue record for this book is available from the National Library of Australia

Contents

Acknowledgement	v
Thank You	vi
Introduction: Staging Asylum, Again Tania Cañas and Caroline Wake	1
Tribunal Kaz Therese, Joe Tan, Aunty Rhonda Dixon-Grovenor, Mahdi Mohammadi, Katie Green, Jawad Yaqoubi and Paul Dwyer	9
ASYLUM Festival	55
Going for Gold Noëlle Janaczewska	61
Three Angry Australians Tania Cañas	69
A Puppet Show for All Ages Georgia Symons	83
We All Know What's Happening Samara Hersch and Lara Thoms	97
The Audition Patricia Cornelius, Tes Lyssiotis, Sahra Davoudi, Christos Tsiolkas, Melissa Reeves, Milad Norouzi and Wahibe Moussa	129

Acknowledgement

To begin, we acknowledge the traditional custodians of the lands on which these plays premiered, and this anthology was edited. Specifically, these plays premiered on the lands of the Gadigal, Dharug, and Wurundjeri peoples, custodians of the places we now call Sydney, Western Sydney, and Melbourne respectively. The anthology was edited on the lands of the Bedegal people of the Eora Nation and Darkinjung country as well as the lands of the Wadawurrung people of the Kulin Nation. We pay our respects to Elders past and present and in doing so acknowledge that sovereignty was never ceded, and that the struggle for justice continues.

The driving principle of this book is to honour that First Nations Peoples, lands, practices and knowledges remain sovereign, regardless of any constitutional recognition, or non-recognition, of this fact. Another principle is that so-called Australia, as a settler-colonial nation-state, subjects Aboriginal and Torres Strait Islanders as well as asylum seekers, refugees, and ex-detainees to different yet interrelated experiences of violence, including incarceration, criminalisation and discrimination. Still another principle is that despite this, the fact remains that displacement and First Nations dispossession are processes which are bound and that even in forced displacement we acknowledge we are on Aboriginal land and land struggles continue to this day.

Thank You

There are many artists and colleagues who have contributed to this book over the years it has taken to research and assemble. They include all those artists who generously shared their work, even when we were not able to include it in the final collection; those whose work is included in the anthology and who have since patiently helped us not only with scripts but also with images, copyright permissions, and introductions; Dr Emma Cox, who edited the first *Staging Asylum* anthology back in 2013, gave us her blessing for a second and remains a leading thinker in the field; our scholar friends who helped us to think through the intersection of theatre and forced displacement, including Dr Danny Butt, members of the Forced Migration Research Network at UNSW, and the Performance of the Real Research Theme at the University of Otago; and our universities for their research support, namely the Faculty of Arts, Design and Architecture at UNSW Sydney. And we thank Currency Press, in particular Claire Grady and her team, for their interest in our project and support throughout the process. Special thanks to Claire for navigating the complex contractual issues associated with multi-authored plays so carefully and caringly.

We also extend our gratitude to friends and family, without whom we could not do this work. Tania would like to thank her famila for their love, solidarity and helping her navigate displacement as resistance. Caroline would like to thank Patrick, Marlon and Frankie, as well as the extended Wake, Haid and Kyriacou clans, for their ongoing support and inspiration.

We dedicate this volume to all who have endured the Australian border regime and continue to resist.

Introduction: Staging Asylum, Again

Tania Cañas and Caroline Wake

In 2013, Currency Press published *Staging Asylum: Contemporary Australian Plays about Refugees*—a collection of six plays that sought to capture the diversity of refugee-related theatre made during the first decade of the 21st century. In her introduction, editor Emma Cox described it as ranging across 'satire to knowing and ironic verbatim theatre, to narratives of trauma and self-inflicted violence derived from asylum seekers' stories, to autobiographical as well as community-devised performance' (Cox 2013, viii). The authors included survivors of immigration detention as well as both white and non-white settlers. Two of the six plays were authored by ensembles: one featured no asylum seekers and the other featured 21 asylum seekers as cast members. Five of the six plays were written and produced in the five years following 2001, a landmark year not only for the September 11 attacks but also for the advent of the Pacific Solution (the sixth play was produced in 2010). Each play 'represent[ed] a perspective on the politics and debates surrounding unauthorised asylum seekers (mostly "boatpeople" ...) in Australia today' (viii). Thus, the book became 'the first collection to recognise ... the role theatre has played in one of Australia's most hotly debated and urgent contemporary issues' (vii).

It is both terrible and incredible that a decade later, another anthology is not only possible but needed. Since 2013 more than 60 additional refugee-related performances have premiered in Australia. Quantity has also produced variety and this body of work includes autobiographical performance, verbatim and documentary plays, fictional plays, stand-up comedy, opera, participatory and immersive performance, live art, performance art, dance and children's theatre. The artists who have led these projects have been based in so-called countries of origin (e.g. Iran), transit (e.g. Indonesia), and destination (e.g. Australia) as well as in countries that have become legal liminal zones because Australia pays them to incarcerate refugees on its behalf (e.g. Papua New Guinea and the Republic of Nauru). Performances made in response to this policy have taken place in detention centres themselves as well as in community halls, small independent theatres, and even the Sydney Opera House. So it is that we find ourselves publishing a companion volume ten years later.

In spite of the central thematic similarity, there are several differences between the two volumes. The first and most obvious is the foregrounding of Indigenous Sovereignty and Aboriginal and Torres Strait Islander ways of working, as seen in the first play of this anthology *Tribunal*. For too long, both scholars and activists ignored the complexities of seeking refuge in the settler-colonial state, often denying Blak[1] Sovereignty and making problematic assumptions about who identifies with the colonial-national 'we' (Levnad 2016). This is despite the fact that, as writer Tony Birch notes, the violence experienced by First Nations peoples and refugees, asylum seekers and ex-detainees stems from the mechanisms of settler-colonialism (Birch 2014). Both experience abuse, incarceration and surveillance by the state (in different yet structurally similar ways) and Aboriginal people also experience displacement (in that they are dispossessed, alienated and without rights 'in our own land') (2014, 206; 200). He argues that Aboriginal people must assert:

> moral authority and ownership of this country. Our legitimacy does not lie within the legal system and is not dependent on state recognition. It lies within ourselves ... We need to claim our rights beyond being stuck in an argument about the dominant culture's view of land rights or identity. And we need to claim and legitimate our authority by speaking out for, and protecting the rights of others, who live in, or visit our country. (Birch 2014, 200–201)

Aboriginal leaders have done just that, as when the late Uncle Ray Jackson—an activist and Wiradjuri Elder—issued Aboriginal passports to asylum seekers and refugees, and when Uncle Robbie Thorpe did the same at RISE's Sovereignty + Sanctuary event (see

---

1. 'Blak' as a term coined by Erub/Mer and K'ua K'ua artist Destiny Deacon. For more information see Munro (2020).

Pugliese 2015; RISE 2016). Similar acts have occurred across so-called Australia. Such acts do two things: first, they insist on belonging and placemaking aligned with Indigenous Sovereignty and liberation struggles; second, they remind audiences that settler-colonialism is ongoing and that even in forced displacement, one becomes part of the dispossession mechanism.

There are several other differences between the two volumes. Whereas Cox wrote of 'hotly debated and urgent contemporary issues', it is arguable that a certain coolness and numbness—even normativity—has set into the general public. The 2022 federal election provided evidence, if more were needed, that how we treat asylum seekers is *not* hotly debated. On the contrary, both major political parties support every aspect of Operation Sovereign Borders, which might otherwise be called Pacific Solution 2.0. When former prime minister Scott Morrison tried to conjure a last-minute scare campaign by releasing details about an approaching boat on the day of the election, the electorate shrugged (Greene 2022). This indifference was also seen two days later when the new Deputy Prime Minister Richard Marles confirmed that the Labor Government had turned away its first asylum seeker boat (Galloway 2022). Even the left-wing Greens support mandatory detention, albeit for a maximum of seven days (Australian Greens 2020). This contrasts with other countries, where immigration detention remains a measure of last rather than first resort (McAdam and Chong 2019, 110). The privileged passivity of both the political class and the general public could not be further from the experience of those who endure these policies as violent, ongoing, daily and lived.

This highlights another difference between the two volumes—their policy backdrops. While *Staging Asylum* captured responses to the policy of the Pacific Solution, this volume records responses to Operation Sovereign Borders. The Pacific Solution is shorthand for a suite of five policies. Two were introduced during the 1990s, and three were implemented in 2001. In the mid-1990s, the Labor Government introduced the immediate and indefinite incarceration of asylum seekers in immigration detention centres. Later that same decade, the Liberal-National Coalition Government announced temporary protection where refugees were granted three- or five-year visas instead of permanent residency. In 2001, the Coalition introduced three more policies: interdiction (the interception and turning back of asylum seeker boats), excision (the legislative removal of Australian island territories from the migration zone) and offshore processing (the payment to Papua New Guinea and the Republic of Nauru to host 'offshore' detention centres, alongside 'onshore' centres in Australia).

From 2008 to 2012, offshore processing was suspended. However, in 2012, it was reinstated along with the more extreme policies that constitute Operation Sovereign Borders. Nowadays, temporary protection visa holders can never apply for permanent protection. Excision includes the entire continent, meaning the mainland itself is excluded from the migration zone. Interdiction involves 'takebacks' (where authorities return people to the country of departure) as well as 'turnbacks' (where they return a boat to a point just outside the territorial sea of the country of departure). Most onshore processing centres were closed while offshore processing segued into regional resettlement (see McAdam and Chong 2019). Most recently, detention centres have shifted into onshore 'alternative places of detention', such as hotels and schools, with private enterprises and public institutions reconstructed as carceral sites of detention and surveillance (Hall 2022).

Beyond politics and policy, there have also been shifts in media technologies, platforms and practices. The Pacific Solution unfolded during the era of email and early mobile phones; in contrast, Operation Sovereign Borders has evolved alongside smartphones and social media. Instead of refugees relying on activists to act as intermediaries— or activists in positions of power appointing themselves to this role— documenting lived experience on communities' own terms has become increasingly possible. So too has direct and immediate communication with the public and potential artistic collaborators. Thus, refugee activism has shifted the social-political practices and norms of platforming.

This shift in who speaks can be seen in authorship patterns. While four of the six plays in *Staging Asylum* were sole-authored works, here the ratios are more even: the three full-length plays are devised by an ensemble and the three short plays are sole-authored. *Tribunal*, for instance, was conceived by artist Kaz Therese and human rights lawyer Joe Tan, and co-devised with a cast that included Aunty

Rhonda Dixon-Grovenor, a Gadigial/Bidgigal/Darug/Yuin Elder, and two members of the refugee community, a former Red Cross worker and an academic. Performed in English, Darug and Hazaragi—both of which went untranslated—the play also challenged the Anglophone monolingualism of mainstream Australian theatre.

Then there is *We All Know What's Happening*, conceived by Samara Hersch and Lara Thoms, who led seven young people to devise a show in response to the incarceration of refugee children their age. Lastly, there is *The Audition*, authored by seven playwrights: four established, three emerging and all with first- or second-generation experiences of migration.

While the response to the Pacific Solution was dominated by documentary plays, as exemplified by *CMI (A Certain Maritime Incident)* in the first volume, the response to Operation Sovereign Borders has been more theatrically adventurous and formally diverse. Documentary modes have not been abandoned completely, which is why we include *Tribunal* and, if the volume were bigger, could have included Hillary Bell's *Flying Fish Cove* (2015), Ross Mueller's *Darker Angels* (2015), or Katie Green's *If You Come to Australia* (2015). However, we also include it because it represents a new genre of what we might call decolonial theatre, which seeks to place the experiences of asylum seekers and refugees alongside those of Aboriginal and Torres Strait Islanders. Other examples include Keg de Souza's installation *Redfern School of Displacement* (2016) and Marrugeku's production *Jurrungu Ngan-ga [Straight Talk]* (2022).

Another new genre that has emerged is theatre made by, with and about children, represented here by *We All Know What's Happening* but also apparent in Treehouse Theatre's series of works (2010 onwards), Sandra Thibodeaux's *The Age of Bones* (Zaman Belulang, 2016), Duncan Graham's *Amphibian* (2018), and Jay Emmanuel's *Children of the Sea* (2021). Metatheatre is also a strong trend, represented here by Georgia Symons' *A Puppet Show for All Ages* and *The Audition* and also evident in Dhananjaya Karunarathne's *A Sri Lankan Tamil Asylum Seeker's Story as Performed by Australian Actors Under the Guidance of a Sinhalese Director* (2015) and The Last Great Hunt's *All That Glitters* (2015). Comedy, too, has been more visible, seen here in Noëlle Janaczewska's *Going for Gold* and Tania Cañas' *Three*

Angry Australians and elsewhere in Tony Robertson's satire *Sentinel Chickens* (2014) and Tom Ballard's stand-up show *Boundless Plains to Share* (2016).

Perhaps the most profound shift has been in the dramaturgy of presence, absence and distance. Whereas earlier efforts were concerned with giving refugees a presence on the Australian stage—whether through casting, borrowing words and stories, reproducing images, or having actors serve as their surrogates—now artists are more concerned with absence and distance. Each play circles around this absence in a slightly different way. *Tribunal* concludes with the image of a friend still held in detention; *A Puppet Show for All Ages* stages an intimate tussle between a refugee who has taken over the body of an actor and the performer who tries to eject her; both *Going for Gold* and *Three Angry Australians* feature Australians talking about other Australians and finish in subdued silence; *We All Know What's Happening* has a stage full of microphone stands representing those same children; and *The Audition* closes with the line 'I'm the only girl left in here from my boat'. In this way, theatre's role has shifted. During the Pacific Solution, the emphasis was on documenting abuse and raising awareness. Ten years later, documentation abounds—there are scores of reports, hundreds of images, thousands of posts—so there is a greater emphasis on critique, whether of advocates, the nation-state or theatre itself.

Staging Asylum, Again reflects these shifts in the ethos of the publication. Taking our cue from the artists, we have sought to emulate their ethic of care by prioritising co-authorship models, including detailed artist statements, and collaborating with them on introductions. The anthology offers a snapshot of moments, resistances and critical changes at the intersection of theatre and displacement. Though we were only able to include six works, they represent hundreds of people and performances locally and internationally. And for all of their variety, these plays are bound by a common conviction that theatre is profoundly political, not only because it responds to the headlines but because it borrows the materials of this world to craft the image of another. *Staging Asylum, Again* offers a glimpse of alternative possibilities and imaginings—of how things could and should be otherwise.

References

Australian Greens. 2020. *Immigration and Refugees*. ACT: Australian Greens. https://greens.org.au/policies/immigration-and-refugees.

Birch, Tony. 2014. 'The Last Refuge of the 'Un-Australian''. In *History, Power, Text: Cultural Studies and Indigenous Studies*, edited by Timothy Neale, Crystal McKinnon and Eve Vincent, 198–207. Sydney: University of Technology Sydney ePress. https://doi.org/10.5130/978-0-9872369-1-3.m

Cox, Emma. 2013. 'Introduction: Knowing Strangers'. In *Staging Asylum: Contemporary Plays About Refugees*, edited by Emma Cox, vii–x. Strawberry Hills: Currency Press.

Galloway, Anthony. 2022. 'Albanese Government Turns Around Its First Asylum Seeker Boat'. *Sydney Morning Herald*, 24 May. https://www.smh.com.au/politics/federal/albanese-government-turns-around-its-first-asylum-seeker-boat-20220524-p5ao2y.html.

Greene, Andrew. 2022. 'Election Day's Asylum Boat'. *ABC AM*, 27 May. https://www.abc.net.au/radio/programs/am/election-days-asylum-boat/13902120.

Hall, Bianca. 2022. 'Government Fights to Keep List of Secret Detention Sites from Public'. *Sydney Morning Herald*, 20 July. https://www.smh.com.au/national/government-fights-to-keep-list-of-secret-detention-sites-from-public-20220720-p5b2zt.html.

Levnad, Sam. 2016. 'Migrant Justice in Settler-Colonial Australia'. *Arena Magazine*, April. https://arena.org.au/migrant-justice-in-settler-colonial-australia-by-sam-levnad/.

McAdam, Jane and Fiona Chong. 2019. *Refugee Rights and Policy Wrongs: A Frank, Up-to-Date Guide by Experts*. Sydney: UNSW Press.

Munro, Kate L. 2020. 'Why "Blak" not Black?: Artist Destiny Deacon and the Origins of this Word'. *NITV*, 29 June. https://www.sbs.com.au/nitv/article/why-blak-not-black-artist-destiny-deacon-and-the-origins-of-this-word/7gv3mykzv.

Pugliese, Joseph. 2015. 'Geopolitics of Aboriginal Sovereignty: Colonial Law as 'a Species of Excess of Its Own Authority', Aboriginal Passport

Ceremonies and Asylum Seekers'. *Law Text Culture* 19: 84–115. https://ro.uow.edu.au/ltc/vol19/iss1/4.

RISE. 2016. 'Sovereignty + Sanctuary: A First Nations / Refugee Solidarity Event'. *RISE. Refugees, Survivors and Ex-Detainees*, 15 June. https://www.riserefugee.org/sovereignty-sanctuary/.

TRIBUNAL

*Kaz Therese, Joe Tan, Aunty Rhonda Dixon-Grovenor,
Mahdi Mohammadi, Katie Green,
Jawad Yaqoubi and Paul Dwyer*

Aunty Rhonda Dixon-Grovenor in PYT Fairfield and Griffin Theatre's TRIBUNAL, 2016 (Photo: Alex Wisser)

Introduction

For as long as there have been immigration detention centres, there have been calls for a royal commission (e.g., Flanagan 2017; Haigh 2018; Project Safecom 2005). In the ongoing absence of one, citizens have stepped into the breach. In 2005, academics held their own people's inquiry into immigration detention, later publishing the results in *Human Rights Overboard: Seeking Asylum in Australia* (Briskman, Latham and Goddard 2008). Roughly a decade later, Sydney's PYT Fairfield (PYT) and Griffin Theatre Company (Griffin) co-produced *Tribunal*. However, whereas previous people's inquiries sought to reproduce colonial law, this performance sought to interrogate it and to model other possibilities. For how legitimate can colonial law be when it is illegitimately imposed on unceded Aboriginal lands? What might a people's court look like if it were to contest colonial logics of truth, authority and credibility, and focus instead on conversation, multiplicity and ceremony? How might we enact a truth and reconciliation commission that attends to the forced displacement of both First Peoples and asylum seekers? Combining participatory theatre, legal process, embodied histories and occasionally slam poetry, *Tribunal* offers one possible answer to these questions.

The first seeds of the performance go back to 2013 when two artists, Kaz Therese and Boris Bagattini, and human rights lawyer, Joe Tan, undertook a residency at Adhocracy, an annual festival for the 'creative development and critical discussion of experimental, multidisciplinary arts projects' (Vitalstatistix 2023). This early work-in-progress was called *Love and Boats* with a reviewer describing it as 'unconstrained conversation about the intersections which characterise the immigrant experience: love and law, freedom and oppression, integration and isolationism' (Brooker 2013). Therese, who was by now Artistic Director of PYT, had a chance to refine this conversation when they participated in Griffin's Studio program—a creative lab for early- and mid-career artists. The two companies could not be more different: PYT is based in Western Sydney and focuses on the 'development and engagement of local young and emerging artists', while Griffin is based in King's Cross, an inner-city suburb that was once bohemian and is now bourgeois, and focuses on the 'development and staging of new Australian writing' (Arts House 2017; Griffin 2023). To make *Tribunal*, the cast worked slowly over eight months to develop the framework and language of the reimagined tribunal, followed by an intense six-week rehearsal period. Led by Aunty Rhonda Dixon-Grovenor, a Gadigal/Bidgigal/Darug/Yuin Elder, the cast also included Mahdi Mohammadi, a Hazara theatre maker whose application for protection was still underway at the time; Jawad Yaqoubi, a fellow refugee; Katie Green, a former Red Cross worker; Paul Dwyer, an academic, dramaturg and performer; and Therese themself. In this way, the play brought together a multilingual and multigenerational community of artists, activists and refugees.

In August 2016, *Tribunal* opened to a full house at the SBW Stables Theatre, Sydney, before playing in Fairfield in March 2017. The work then played to large houses at Melbourne's Arts House, where it was programmed alongside *We All Know What's Happening* (August 2017), Sydney's Carriageworks (January 2018) and the Sydney Opera House (July 2018). *Tribunal* starts with Dixon-Grovenor already on stage and watching as the audience enters. Once seated, the other performers assume their places behind her before Green stamps her heel twice and orders, 'All rise!'. Dixon-Grovenor then welcomes everyone in Darug language and introduces herself as 'the convenor of this People's Tribunal'. When Mohammadi steps forward to testify to his experiences, he is constantly interrupted by Dwyer, who plays an immigration officer. Finally, Mohammadi stops in frustration and asks, 'Can I just say my own story in my own words?', to which Dixon-Grovenor replies, 'Mahdi, this is a theatre—you can do what you like'. From here, the performance loosens, and the actors who play themselves (Mohammadi, Yaqoubi, Green and Dixon-Grovenor) tell their stories using direct address, photographs, song and dance. Therese plays human rights lawyer Joe Tan, delivering his words in the style of headphone verbatim, and Dwyer plays a series of officials.

In the second act, the mention of the Department of Immigration and Border Protection's Code of Behaviour prompts Dixon-Grovenor to recall the racist *Aboriginal Protection Act* that governed her early life. She speaks of her late grandfather being threatened with a code that would see the loss of his welfare payments if he spoke in language. Similarly, Mohammadi is warned by an immigration officer that deportation could happen at any time, even for a minor traffic offence. He later remarks, 'no more parties', as a neighbour might complain. In this way, *Tribunal* draws parallels between First Peoples and displaced peoples as groups that experienced daily bureaucratic violence through the invention and continual maintenance of Australia as a nation-state. Critic Stephen Pham noted that white surveillance continued despite non-white voices being centred on stage, in the sense that 'while the production visibly engages with non-Whitenesses, Whiteness doesn't disappear: it just goes unacknowledged' (Pham 2016). In contrast, Mohammadi explicitly acknowledges Dixon-Grovenor 'as the owner of this country' and respectfully places an Afghan shawl across her shoulders over her possum skin cloak. This moment models a solidarity that understands nation-state violence against refugees and asylum seekers as an extension of settler-colonialism and Aboriginal dispossession.

Reviewers described *Tribunal* as a 'critical participatory performance' (McIntyre and McLean 2016), 'a ceremony we are all invited to' (Chantiri 2016), a 'gathering' (Weber 2017) and a 'verbatim, anecdotal format' (Wrong 2016)—it is all of this and more. No two performances were ever the same. In Sydney, Dixon-Grovenor's Welcome to Country was woven into the dramaturgy of the event, so that it was not just a necessary formality as it can be on some occasions. In Melbourne, she led an Acknowledgement of Country instead. In some performances, there was a smoking ceremony and a live yidaki (didjeridu) performance. Before, during and after the show, Iraqi tea, coffee and sweets from local businesses were served to the audience. There were also different guest performers each night, who were invited onto the stage for the final scenes and discussions. Often, two young poets joined the stage and did slam poetry about honour and resistance. While it is hard to capture these practices in the script, they speak to Kaz Therese's participatory ethos and deep awareness of context, from supporting local businesses to understanding whose land on which one stands.

The original program for *Tribunal* included a dedication to the '55 asylum seekers who drowned on 10th of June 2013, as we sat in

Adelaide and London developing this work'. During the performance, Mohammadi speaks directly to the audience about young refugees who continue to die, including four 'while we have been making this show'. In a strange coincidence, the performance premiered the same week the Nauru Files—more than 2,000 leaked incident reports from Australia's offshore camps—were released. In contrast to that catalogue of cruelty, *Tribunal* models what Therese calls 'radical kindness' towards refugees and asylum seekers.

Tania Cañas and Caroline Wake

References

Arts House. 2017. 'Tribunal by PYT Fairfield Show Program'. http://www.artshouse.com.au/wp-content/uploads/2017/07/Tribunal-by-PYT-l-Fairfield-Show-Program.pdf.

Briskman, Linda, Susan Latham, and Chris Goddard. 2008. *Human Rights Overboard: Seeking Asylum in Australia.* Melbourne: Scribe.

Brooker, Ben. 2013. 'Shadow Boxing With Illusions'. *RealTime* 116, 19 August. https://www.realtime.org.au/shadow-boxing-with-illusions/.

Chantiri, Gabbi. 2016. 'Playmate: *Tribunal* (Powerhouse Youth Theatre and Griffin Theatre)'. *FBi Radio*, 17 August. https://fbiradio.com/playmate-tribunal-powerhouse-youth-theatre-griffin-theatre/.

Flanagan, Richard. 2017. 'Australia Built a Hell for Refugees on Manus. The Shame Will Outlive Us All'. *The Guardian,* 24 November. https://www.theguardian.com/australia-news/2017/nov/24/the-shame-of-the-evil-being-done-on-manus-will-outlive-us-all.

Griffin Theatre Company. 2023. 'About Us.' *Griffin Theatre Company*, n.d. https://griffintheatre.com.au/about/

Haigh, Bruce. 2018. 'Why We Need a Royal Commission into Asylum-Seeker Policy'. *Canberra Times*, 23 April. https://www.canberratimes.com.au/story/6136586/why-we-need-a-royal-commission-into-asylum-seeker-policy/.

McIntyre, Siân and Laura McLean. 2016. 'Tribunal: A Review'. *RUNWAY: Australian Experimental Arts*, 2 October. https://web.archive.org/web/20161002021616/http://runway.org.au/tribunal-a-review.

Pham, Stephen. 2016. 'Handle with Care: On White Australian Invisibility in Non-White Dialogues'. *The Lifted Brow*, 15 August. https://www.theliftedbrow.com/liftedbrow/handle-with-care-on-white-australian.

Project Safecom. 2005. 'The Royal Commission Call'. *Project Safecom*, 3 May. https://www.safecom.org.au/royal-commission.htm.

Vitalstatistix. 2023. 'Adhocracy 2023'. Vitalstatistix, n.d. https://vitalstatistix.com.au/projects/adhocracy-2023/.

Weber, Kris. 2017. 'Tribunal: A Review'. *Theatre People*, 22 July. https://www.theatrepeople.com.au/tribunal/.

Wrong, Suzy. 2016. 'Review: *Tribunal* (Powerhouse Youth Theatre / Griffin Theatre Company)'. *Suzy Goes See*, 13 August. https://suzygoessee.com/2016/08/13/review-tribunal-powerhouse-youth-theatre-griffin-theatre-company/.

Tribunal premiered in 2016 at the SBW Stables Theatre in Kings Cross as a PYT Fairfield and Griffin Theatre co-production with the following creative team:

Concept, Lead Artist and Creative Producer: Kaz Therese
Concept and Human Rights Lawyer: Joe Tan
Text devised by Kaz Therese, Joe Tan, Aunty Rhonda Dixon-Grovenor, Mahdi Mohammadi, Katie Green, Paul Dwyer and Jawad Yaqoubi
Performed by Aunty Rhonda Dixon-Grovenor, Mahdi Mohammadi, Katie Green, Kaz Therese, Paul Dwyer, Jawad Yaqoubi
Guest speakers/performers: Iman Etri, Bilal Hafda, Zaki Haidari, Tamana Mirzada, Haitham Jaju, Sarah Coconis and others
Text Editor: Paul Dwyer
Outside Eye: Chris Ryan
Design: Province Studio (Laura Pike and Ann Louise Dadak)
Possum Skin Cloak Ceremony and Construction: Senior Yuin Law Man Uncle Max Dulumunmun Harrion, Yarren Dixon, Amanda Jane Reynolds, Vanessa Starzynski, Aunty Rhonda Dixon-Grovenor, Nadeena Dixon, Naryma Dixon, Wasana Dixon, and Province Studio.
Video Design: Sean Bacon
Sound Design: James Brown
Lighting Design: Emma Lockhart-Wilson
Stage Manager/Production Manager: Patrick Howard

Subsequent seasons: PYT Fairfield (2017), Museum of Contemporary Art, Sydney (2017), Arts House, Melbourne (2017), Sydney Festival at Carriageworks (2018), Sydney Opera House (2018).

Acknowledgements

Bec Dean, Brianna Munting, Victoria Spence, PYT Board Members, The Parents' Café, Layla and Firas Naji, Oliver Slewa, Fairfield IEC, pvi collective, Callum, Ruth Sugden, Boris Bagattini, Emma Webb, Lee Lewis, Will Harvey, Ben Winspear, Grace Partridge, Josipa Draisma.

We also gratefully acknowledge funding and in-kind support from the Australia Council for the Arts, Create NSW, Vitalstatistix (Adhocracy 2013), Griffin Theatre, University of Sydney (Department of Theatre and Performance Studies), and University of Wollongong.

Artist's Statement

During a three-day research residency, an asylum seeker boat capsized off Australia's coast in international waters. This led to a catastrophic series of systemic failures where 55 people died. I was in residence with video artist Boris Bagattini and human rights lawyer Joe Tan (on Skype via London) for a project idea titled 'Love and Boats' which became *Tribunal*. We were all stunned, and sat together for hours talking, trying to make sense of things. I remember asking Joe, 'How do we change everything? What do we need to do to stop this from happening?' He replied, 'In Australia we need to have a Truth and Reconciliation Tribunal to tell the true histories of Australia.'

At the time, the debate on gay marriage was raging across Australia and as a queer person I had witnessed weddings where ritual and ceremonies were held without being 'legal'. This notion of creating ceremony, regardless of law, was exciting to me and I thought that we could stage a tribunal as a performance, a ceremony and a political act to create change.

I started to furiously research tribunals, the shape and form of them, their processes and achievements. In other global tribunals, the tribunal itself was a curated collection of lawyers, artists, survivors, human rights activists, philosophers ... I was inspired to start building a collective of peers to form an Australian tribunal as a performative action.

In 2016 I became a Studio Artist at Griffin Theatre and began the conversation around presenting a new work, *Tribunal*. Griffin supported a research trip to the Middle East for five weeks, where I met and spoke with theatre makers, activists, academics and theologians from both Israel and Palestine, discussing their ideas, obstacles and active pathways for peace. These pathways often included intergenerational strategies of connection such as creating conversation through sharing a meal, inviting young people and children to come together for games and storytelling, theatre companies dedicated to reconciliation through storytelling and conversation. I was reminded of the work of Lois Weaver's *Long Table*, a public address system that utilises nonhierarchical spaces for conversation about difficult subjects. These elements led to me developing a new kind of process for creating theatre.

This process enabled a slowing of time and shared space, creating cultural and psychological safety for the team and participants, and ensured people from diverse classes, cultures and experiences could come together, finding kind ways to talk about difficult subjects and create a genuinely radical new performance work.

To all the artists, thank you. To Aunty Rhonda, thank you for continuing to evolve this work within your cultural leadership as a Gadigal/Bidgigal Elder of the Eora Nation.

Lots of love,
Kaz

Foreword

The *Tribunal* came to me over a series of many dreams which began in 2001 when the 'Pacific Solution' of detaining asylum seekers on remote offshore islands was first conceived and implemented by an Australian Government that prioritised their electoral success over the lives of the most vulnerable, traumatised and desperate human beings.

The most visceral element of many of those dreams involved the boat. I began to understand the linear connections between temporal points, and the searing, visceral image of the boat was common to three groups of people who shared an uneasy co-existence in country. The boat symbolises a common trauma suffered by the original Indigenous inhabitants of Australia as they watched the detritus of Victorian England being conveyed to their shores in the first and subsequent fleets dating from 1788. Over 200 years later, the descendants of those convicts are this time 'the invaded' as boatloads of refugees recreate history. The symbolism of the boat, and the ensuing genocidal acts of violent dispossession were imprinted in the DNA of the nation and deeply terrorised its peoples. This fear explained the gross overreaction of a White Australia which has never yet reconciled with Black Australia over the ancestral misdeeds of its forebears.

While representing refugee clients on the island of Nauru, I had the opportunity of realising my dream of materialising this arc of history in a production that provided a vessel for an amazing collective of artists to inject their own dreams, realities and shared experiences. Shortly after, I fled Australia for England, burnt out and suffering the effects of years of secondary trauma from working at the frontline, reversing the flow of convicts and refugees to that colonial outpost.

Through some cruel irony, the UK Home Office retained my passport to process my visa and I was detained on my new island for seven months, unable to leave to watch the play premiere in Sydney. To this day, I have not seen a live version of the production.

In 2021, I declined an offer to publish the play. Barely a year later, and the UK Government announced its 'Rwanda Solution', the mechanism that would enable asylum seekers intercepted while crossing the

English Channel to be removed to Rwanda for the processing of their protection claims. Very sadly, human beings have shown an inclination not to learn the lessons of history.

The transitional justice catchcry of '*nunca más!*' (never again) in the aftermath of inquiries into the enforced disappearances under the Argentinian military dictatorship was premised on the publication of the written findings of a National Commission. I realised the only way we would ever have our 'never again' moment would be if our People's Tribunal could be memorialised in some form. Furthermore, it dawned on me that it wasn't just *my* dreams (and nightmares) but the dreaming of the Cabrogal people of the Darug Nation and other First Peoples, the many refugees who have suffered and survived under a relentless and cruel policy, and the amazing artists who participated in this production under Kaz's leadership, care and vision.

I commend this publication in the hope it will inspire others to realise their own versions or maybe even allow another live production of this very play that I will actually be able to experience. One can only dream!

Joe Tan

CHARACTERS

The *Tribunal* cast, for the most part, present a version of themselves on stage in a text that is composed of documentary sources and autobiographical materials, including private archival photographs, first-person monologues, transcriptions of conversations between members of the creative team, and so on. In order of appearance, these cast members are:

AUNTY RHONDA DIXON-GROVENOR, First Nations Elder and Convenor of the Tribunal.

KATIE GREEN, a lawyer, formerly a caseworker for a refugee support agency.

MAHDI MOHAMMADI, a theatre and film director from Kabul, Afghanistan; living in Australia on a temporary protection visa and working as a bricklayer.

JAWAD YAQOUBI, a friend of Mahdi; living in Australia on a permanent protection visa and working as a bricklayer.

PAUL DWYER, a university lecturer (plays the Immigration Officer and other government officals).

KAZ THERESE, an interdisciplinary artist, director and curator (plays themself but also delivers the words of their friend, JOE TAN, a human rights lawyer).

DESIGN AND SETTING

The setting for *Tribunal* is the 'here and now' of whatever theatre space the work is being performed in. The stage space is lightly 'dressed': a Persian-style carpet on the floor covers a large part of centre stage. Upstage left of the carpet, there are three wooden chairs and, upstage right, another three wooden chairs. Collectively, these chairs make a kind of V-shape, opening up to the audience. In most venues, Aunty Rhonda sits in an upholstered chair at the apex of this V. There are AV projections on an upstage screen (or, in a smaller space, the back walls of the theatre). In a larger theatre, the space upstage is delimited by a 'wall of bureaucracy', i.e. dozens of archive boxes stacked in a somewhat random, grid-like structure.

PRE-SHOW

On the opening night of each new season, PYT Fairfield and other presenters will work with Elders to arrange a pre-show smoking ceremony outside, or in the foyer of, the theatre. If the work is being performed on lands other than those of the Gadigal, Darug, Bidjigal or Yuin peoples (from which AUNTY RHONDA DIXON-GROVENOR, *the 'Convenor' of the Tribunal, is descended), advice on cultural protocols will be sought from the local group of Elders, including their views about* AUNTY RHONDA *opening the show in her traditional language. If appropriate, a local Elder can open the show with* AUNTY RHONDA.

At the end of the smoking ceremony, Front of House staff invite the audience to make their way silently into the theatre space.

WELCOME / OPENING OF THE TRIBUNAL

AUNTY RHONDA DIXON-GROVENOR *is onstage, in her possum skin ceremonial cloak. As the final audience members settle into their seats,* KATIE GREEN, PAUL DWYER, KAZ THERESE *and* JAWAD YAQOUBI *enter and stand upstage of* AUNTY RHONDA.

KATIE: All rise!

> KATIE *gestures for audience members to stand. If need be, she repeats the instruction until they do.*

AUNTY RHONDA: [*speaking in Gadigal/Darug language*]
Warami Gadigal/Darug Nura wellamabami
inyina Byalla-wa
guyanayallung
Budyari darra/burra
Yanu

KATIE: The Tribunal is now in session. Be seated.

> AUNTY RHONDA *stays standing; audience members and other performers sit.*

AUNTY RHONDA: Welcome. My name is Aunty Rhonda Dixon-Grovenor. I am a descendant of the Gadigal people of the Sydney area, the Bidjigal people of La Perouse area, also the Darug people from out west, and the Yuin people from the far south coast of New South Wales. The possum is my Darug totem. This possum skin cloak is used in different ceremonies such as births, deaths, marriages, or healing ceremonies …

Tonight, I am the convenor of this People's Tribunal—a place where we gather to bear witness to the stories of asylum seekers and refugees, to acknowledge the hurt and damage that they are suffering. We also acknowledge their strength, their resilience, their joy, and creativity.

All the people speaking here tonight are speaking their truth from their own personal experiences. And you will also have a chance to speak if you wish.

This land that we are standing on here today is Aboriginal land. The government's treatment of asylum seekers brings me—and many other Aboriginal people I have spoken to—sadness and grief. It is a matter of great concern. This is not our culture, to treat people this way.

MAHDI MOHAMMADI *enters and appears before* AUNTY RHONDA, *holding a traditional Afghan scarf as a gift.*

MAHDI: [*speaking in Hazaragi, the form of Persian dialect used by most Hazara people from Afghanistan*] I request permission to appear before the Tribunal.

AUNTY RHONDA *signals for him to step forward.*

[*In Hazaragi*] I bring this scarf to you from my country as a gift to acknowledge you as the owner of this country.

AUNTY RHONDA *nods and* MAHDI *steps closer, carefully placing the Afghan scarf around her shoulders, partly overlapping the possum skin cloak.* AUNTY RHONDA *opens her arms and they hug.* PAUL *immediately launches into the next scene …*

INTERVIEW SCENE

PAUL/IMMIGRATION OFFICER: Commencing arrival and induction interview with NR Number Zero-Three-Two.

This interview is being conducted between myself, an officer of the Department of Immigration and Border Protection, and Mohammadi … ah, sorry, Mahdi … Mohammadi.

I need information about you and your arrival in Australia. This interview will be recorded. You have the assistance of an interpreter.

JAWAD *stands up and translates into Hazaragi the gist of what Paul has said.*

This interview is your opportunity to provide any reasons why you should not be removed from Australia.

JAWAD *translates in Hazaragi ...*

You should understand that if the information you give at any future interview is different from what you tell me now, this could raise doubts about the reliability of what you have said.

JAWAD *translates in Hazaragi ...*

This information will not be made available to authorities in the country of your habitual residence.

JAWAD *translates in Hazaragi ...*

The exception to this is if a determination is made that you have no lawful basis to remain in Australia.

JAWAD *translates in Hazaragi ...*

Do you understand what I have said?

JAWAD *translates in Hazaragi ...*

MAHDI: [*in English*] Yes
PAUL/IMMIGRATION OFFICER: Do you understand the interpreter?

JAWAD *translates in Hazaragi ...*

MAHDI: [*in English*] Yes.
PAUL/IMMIGRATION OFFICER: Now what's your date of birth?

JAWAD *translates in Hazaragi ...*

MAHDI *starts giving a long explanation in Hazaragi ...* JAWAD *starts interjecting, asking questions and making comments of his own ... eg. 'So the date of birth on your passport was wrong because it was a fake passport, is that it?' ...* PAUL *signals to* JAWAD *impatiently ...* JAWAD *cuts* MAHDI *off and gives the date ...*

JAWAD: [*in English*] Eleventh of June 1990.

PAUL/IMMIGRATION OFFICER: Now where were you born? What village or city, and in what province?

    JAWAD *translates in Hazaragi* ...

MAHDI: [*in Hazaragi*] I was born in Mashad, a city in Iran, in Khorasaan Province.
JAWAD: [*in English*] I was born in Mashad, city of Iran, Khorasaan Province.
PAUL/IMMIGRATION OFFICER: Okay—and that's in Iran?
JAWAD: [*in English*] Yes
PAUL/IMMIGRATION OFFICER: Okay, now are you a citizen of any other country?

    JAWAD *translates in Hazaragi* ...

MAHDI: [*in Hazaragi*] Yes, I am an Afghan citizen.
JAWAD: [*in English*] I am Afghan citizen.
MAHDI: [*breaks into English, addresses the audience*] ... Stop! Please. These interviews go on for hours and hours. They never show any concern about what you've been through. They never let you tell your story in your own words ...

    He turns to AUNTY RHONDA.

Can I just say my own story in my own words?
AUNTY RHONDA: Mahdi, this is a theatre—you can do what you like.
MAHDI: Thank you.

MAHDI SPEAKS OF HIS CHILDHOOD IN IRAN

MAHDI *moves into a more relaxed storytelling mode for this part of his 'testimony'. Throughout his story, as appropriate, images are projected onto a screen or onto the wall upstage: street scenes from Mashad, Iran; the World Trade Centre; old family photographs; the mountains around Kabul, etc.*

MAHDI: I was born in Mashad, Iran, in 1990.
    I grew up and studied there as an Afghan person ... Being Afghan means a lot in Iran—they treat us like we are dirty or useless. Some of them treated us worse than animals. This was my experience as I was growing up in Iran.
    Originally, I'm a Hazara and Hazara people are—

In Hazaragi, MAHDI *asks* JAWAD *to help him find the right words:* '*How do I explain Hazara to them?*'

JAWAD: [*in English, to the audience*] Hazara people are an ethnic minority in Afghanistan. Many of us are persecuted by the Taliban, which is why our families moved to Iran.

MAHDI: Right. But as a kid, I didn't even know that I was Hazara or what is Hazara. All I got was 'you're a dirty Afghan'. Forget it!

Let's talk about my family ... My family is huge—my father, his two wives and twelve children. Together, fifteen people! Our breakfast, lunch, dinner looked like we are having a party. My father—the leader of the family—would sit always in front—

MAHDI *kneels on the floor.*

—and watch that everyone is present.

Then my brothers were usually sitting on both sides and my sisters at the end. Here they are.

MAHDI *names all his siblings, pointing to the place on the floor where they would sit.*

Then my two mothers would come in with a big pot and sit beside my father and start serving food. My mother used to put food in the bowl and my other mother used to pass it around but first my father—

Oh, I forgot to say that if someone was missing for dinner, they would be questioned by my father and even punished ... I remember that one night I was playing outside and missed dinner. My punishment was that I didn't get any food. So, I went to bed hungry. But my mother—I better say 'my inspiration in life'—she gave me some food and I sat in the kitchen, eating my food with fear that my father would catch me. This was life in Iran.

I remember when the September Eleven incident happened. My father was watching TV and I was watching. As a kid, I had no idea how big is that incident. Then America attacked Taliban in Afghanistan.

A few months after, I saw my mother is crying, and I asked her what happened, and she said 'Afghanistan is free now.' My country and your country is free, the place that you belong to.

I had a strange feeling that time, like I felt 'wow, I have a place that I could say: 'I'm from here''. As a thirteen years boy, I cried with my mother. After that, my father decided we should go back to our country.

We were not ready to go but he was the leader, like the president of our family, so we had to accept and we moved back to Afghanistan.

MAHDI bows to AUNTY RHONDA. *She nods and* MAHDI *takes a seat upstage.*

KATIE TENDERS A DOCUMENT

KATIE GREEN *now stands and moves to centre stage. She acknowledges* AUNTY RHONDA *with a bow.*

KATIE: Aunty Rhonda, I'd like to tender this document.

She hands AUNTY RHONDA *the transcript of a statement written by Khodayar Amini, an Afghan Hazara refugee.*

AUNTY RHONDA: Yes, that's fine Katie. Please step forward.

KATIE: [*reading Khodayar Amini's statement*] 'I, Khodayar Amini, write the following few sentences with my blood for those apathetic so-called human beings …

'They did this to me, with slogans of humanity, sentenced me to death. My crime was that I was a refugee. They tortured me for thirty-seven months and during all these times they treated me in the most cruel and inhumane way. They violated my basic human right and took away my human dignity with their false and so-called humane slogans.

'I write this statement with my blood for those who call themselves human beings, I ask you to stand up for the rights of refugees and stop people being killed just because they have become refugees. Humanity is not a slogan; every human being has the right to live. Living shouldn't be a crime anymore. Red Cross, Immigration and the Police killed me with their slogans of humanity and cruel treatments.

'Are there rule of law, social justice and human dignity in this country? If there is, why your behaviour is in contradictory to human rights? I was harassed, incarcerated, taken to court, tortured for eleven months inside immigration detention centre. What was my crime? How your treatment is different from the treatment of the Taliban and Daesh? For three years, you have tortured me in every way. What do you want from us? What's our crime? In your view, we are not human beings.'

KATIE *continues in her own words, explaining the context of this document.*

On Sunday, eighteenth of October 2015, Mr Khodayar Amini, the writer of this text, drove into the bush on the outskirts of Dandenong. He made a video call to refugee advocates who had been trying to support him with his deteriorating mental health. Mr Amini doused himself in petrol and set himself alight on camera. He was dead within minutes.

Pause.

I had met Khodayar a few weeks earlier. He was a client of the Red Cross, where I was working at the time. I remember that there was a special protocol in place if he phoned or turned up at the office, because he often presented as extremely angry or distressed. He wasn't an easy person to work with. I understand what he means when he lumps the Red Cross in with the Immigration Department and the police. We always tried to do our best but sometimes it felt like I was a cog in a system that was destroying people.

KATIE *has finished her testimony and sits down.*

A moment of deep silence.

AUNTY RHONDA *stands to sing the lullaby 'Mama Warrunno'; other performers stand with her.*

AUNTY RHONDA: The reason I chose to sing 'Mama Warrunno' is because all the little children, all the babies, all the Guthers and all the Jarjums that are born, they are all special. Every human being is special and unique.

THE LAWYER AND HIS REFUGEE CLIENTS: PART ONE

The theatre lights are quite dark now, as if it's night time. KAZ *begins to speak from their seat upstage.*

KAZ: I'm in a car in the back streets of Glebe. Paul's there too. It's late on a Sunday night. It's hot, stifling, like thirty-eight degrees. We're talking with a friend of mine, a human rights lawyer, on speaker phone from London.

KAZ: [*stands*] Aunty Rhonda, can I admit this story as hearsay evidence?

AUNTY RHONDA: Yes, Kaz, you may.

KAZ: Thank you. My friend is telling us about a case that kind of broke him. It's part of why he felt he had to leave Australia. It's tricky—for all sorts of reasons—for him to talk about this stuff but he let me make a recording of our conversation in the car. And I'm going to voice his story for you now while I'm listening to the recording.

> KAZ *places a pair of headphones over their ears and presses play on their iPod. For the rest of this scene, they 'relay' to the audience the words of their friend, Joe Tan, a human rights lawyer, reproducing as closely as possible the rhythms, pitch and stresses of his speech.*

KAZ/JOE: So, there was a father, a mother, and two boys ... and I remember going up to RACS [Refugee Advice and Casework Service] one day, which is just around the corner from our office, and going there for a first interview with them and I basically broke down after hearing their story and I realised that I had to do something for them.

They were on SIEV 4, which was the Children Overboard boat— ... so very shortly after Tampa, the whole Tampa fiasco. They were taken to Christmas Island first for processing and then sent straight to PNG onto Manus. They stayed on Manus for about two years, until it was overcrowded ... So my family ended up going to Nauru.

Those areas, like, on PNG, Manus and Nauru became, sort of, Australia's Guantanamo Bays. It was like this legal vacuum where there's no law really operating, and the Australian Government could do what they want with the refugees and no-one heard anything. There was no media scrutiny, no accountability by any branch of government over what was happening in the detention centres.

The mother was having a particularly hard time ... with the other women in the camp ... but then the thing that, the thing that really became prominent for them was that one day [her youngest child] was playing, umm ... and he was called into ... there was ... a fellow detainee, an adult who had sort of enticed him to the computer room on Nauru and, umm, so the little boy went into the computer room with this man, umm, and was basically shown some porn and, umm, after a while when the mother, she, ah, was s—looking for her son—she was hanging out the washing or something—and the little boy ... came out very distressed, crying, and he had semen on his pants.

She basically, from that moment on just lost the plot and developed various mental illnesses ... She would be just washing all day till her hands, kind of the skin on her hands, were just like, would just peel from all the bleaches and detergent that she used ... The little boy also became, also got, got post-traumatic stress disorder and, ah, when I met him he was basically mute, he hardly spoke a word ...

And for two years, they basically tried to get the authorities on Manus—on Nauru, sorry—to do something about this case and get some justice ... but basically they sort of shov—shoved it under the carpet ... and the ... the perpetrator, after a year ... was placed in the same part of the camp as ... the young boy and the rest of the family and so ... that exacerbated the condition again ...

But eventually the, after four or five years, there was a political situation where [Immigration Minister] Vanstone was with all, you know, scores of asylum seekers, main—mainly men who were becoming so, umm, who were self-harming and becoming and—really ser—, a really serious situation, I mean, yeah, the World Health Organisation stepped in and said 'You've got to get these people medevaced back to the mainland' ... And so my family was one of them. And they came to Australia but they never forgot about, you know, the lack of justice that they were afforded to their son on Nauru and decided that they wanted to bring a compensation claim against the government for what had happened. And that's when I stepped in.

> KAZ *removes the headphones from their ears, bows to* AUNTY RHONDA, *and resumes their seat upstage. A deep pause.*

MAHDI TALKS ABOUT STUDYING AND MAKING THEATRE IN KABUL

AUNTY RHONDA: Mahdi, could you tell us a little bit more about yourself?

MAHDI: Sure. So, when I finished Year Twelve of high school, I was deciding what subject I would love to study at the University of Kabul. I knew it was art. My parents wanted for me to be a doctor or an engineer or something, but I loved the arts inside of my body.

In Afghanistan, when you apply for university, you can put down ten choices. So, I put Medicine as first preference—I was sure that I'm not going to get that—and then I put Fine Arts second. I tell my father that Arts was my tenth choice but that my marks were not good so it was the only course I could do. He was saying: 'What is Art? It's not a good choice. It's all about dancing. It's sinful. You should study one more year and take the exam again.' I said: 'It's not all about dance. We will make good things. Like, Islamic stories.' He said: 'Okay, we will see.'

So, in my first year I studied directing for theatre and cinema. It was all Shakespeare, Chekhov, Bertolt Brecht and we watched every movie that ever got an Academy Award. The first one was *Perfume* which has a few naked scenes. I was shocked. Because normally this is censored by government. Our teachers were taking a risk.

And there were girls at university. It was my first time where it was mixed. People were shy but happy. We feel a bit free. If you liked someone, and you were cheeky, you might drop a piece of paper with your phone number on their desk. They might give it to the teacher, in which case you get punished. Or they might phone you. If a boy and a girl are talking on the phone, they have to be careful. If the girl's family finds out, they will hurt you.

JAWAD: One time I was just talking to this girl, just talking—her brother bashed me really badly; I had blood all over my face.

JAWAD gets up and starts circling around MAHDI in this next bit of story.

MAHDI: For us, a first date is like you go for a walk and the boy and girl are like one hundred metres away from each other …

JAWAD: On opposite sides of the street, talking on the phone …

MAHDI: If you are really brave, you might say: 'Hey, do you see that tree? Come under that tree. Just one kiss. Please'.

JAWAD: You might have to wait an hour, even two hours, until you are sure that there is no-one who can see you …

MAHDI and JAWAD come together …

MAHDI: But if you get just one kiss on the cheek—

MAHDI gives JAWAD a quick little kiss on the cheek.

—you will be happy for the whole week.

JAWAD: But if the girl's family catch you, you might be killed.

MAHDI: That's true.

When I was starting the last year of my theatre degree, I met this girl—a very experienced actor.

Photographs of MAHDI's former theatre colleagues, and of their shows, are projected during this next section. MAHDI refers to them as appropriate, highlighting some details.

We decided to make a theatre group with her two sisters. We called ourselves Papyrus Theatre Company. Here we are deciding our artistic program—we chose to work just for women's rights.

We did our first show for the seventh National Festival of Afghan Theatre. This is our slogan—

He mimics a gesture used by all the performers in one of the photos.

'Fight'—it just means 'you must fight'. The people loved this show. It was all movement and dance. Some people cried. They felt the problems we showed. But on national TV, four mullahs spoke about our show and said: 'They must be stopped. They are bringing western culture'. We didn't care because we were so happy, and we were proud and really committed.

Sometimes it was hard to get the women to come to the theatre. I had to lie to their husbands and say 'Oh, I am the manager of this NGO and these women from our organisation are taking your wife to the women's garden—it's just for women—so they can have a special picnic. There will be no men'. But then actually it was our actors who brought the other women to the garden and that's where we performed our show for them. And, of course, as the director, I was there too, and discussed their rights.

This is the show we did for that project. It was in the Women's Prison, in Kabul, so it was just for the women. I wasn't there. This performance was about how you can't just wait for your rights—you have to go and get your rights.

So, this one … Our group had a tour to India and this is a really famous dance of Hazara women. We call it 'Pishpo' and it's really hard. The women dance like this—

He tries to demonstrate.

And you go into more details, and it gets harder and harder and goes for over an hour. Yeah, it's really hard. The men's dance is easier: we just go like this—

He demonstrates.

This is a performance we did in a girl's school—as you can see, it's all girls—and this was about the problems between Hazara and Pashtun and Tajik people. The performance was called 'Peace is Life'. It was about how we have to find a way to live together in peace. We are all human.

So, we had projects with the American Embassy. We performed for International Women's Day. We worked with UN Women, the British Council. All these Western organisations were encouraging us …

Harsh segue back into the lighting state from the earlier scene of MAHDI's *immigration induction interview …*

PAUL/IMMIGRATION OFFICER: Why did you leave your country of nationality?

MAHDI: Three women from our troupe were invited to Sweden and the BBC produced a story about our group. It showed them dancing

which goes against the sharia beliefs. Some extreme religious people saw this and called me an infidel. That's like a sentence to death. That's why I'm seeking asylum from your country.
PAUL/IMMIGRATION OFFICER: Were you specifically threatened?
MAHDI: Yes. Once they came to arrest me. They ambushed us. One of my relatives died.

> *Lights fade.* MAHDI *and* PAUL *sit. Cross-fade into the next piece of* KATIE*'s 'testimony'* ...

A 'DAY IN THE LIFE' OF A RED CROSS WORKER

KATIE: Case work is all about knowing the system and knowing how to navigate it. I've worked in women's refuges, youth refuges, drug and alcohol services ... I know how to find emergency accommodation; I know how to help people access health care; if someone needs to catch a train to visit family in the country for a funeral—I know how to arrange that stuff.

But when I started working with asylum seekers at the Red Cross, I learned how racist the system can be. You want to get a bed in a refuge for a homeless young asylum seeker, they tell you 'Not Eligible for This Service'—refugees are the responsibility of the Department of Immigration. Same with a lot of schools—not eligible; wrong class of visa—or they expect asylum seeker parents to enrol their kids as international students and pay thousands of dollars.

Until 2015, asylum seekers on bridging visas had no right to work. This effectively forced them onto a government benefit. They were given an allowance: eighty-nine per cent of the basic Centrelink benefit. That's four hundred and fifty dollars a fortnight. You hear rumours sometimes about asylum seekers getting free government housing. It's crap. We're talking four hundred and fifty dollars a fortnight to cover food, transport, rent, the lot. I would visit my clients at home and find twelve people living in a three-bedroom house—that was normal.

AUNTY RHONDA: Katie, could you just tell us what a typical day is like for a Red Cross worker?
KATIE: There was no typical day—my job changed as quickly as the policies did. During the Rudd/Gillard administration, there was

this window where asylum seekers were still being released from detention and allowed into the community. So every two weeks, usually Thursday, Immigration would send us a spreadsheet with details of thirty, fifty, seventy people, whatever, being released from detention.

> PAUL *stands and points to the following places with a laser pointer on a map projected onto the screen.*

Planes would be coming from all over the country—Scherger in Far North Queensland, Curtin up in Northern WA, Wickham Point in Darwin—and we would have to be at the airport to pick these people up. Total chaos—a logistical nightmare.

For the asylum seekers who've got family they can stay with, you've gotta do the ring-around and make sure someone's going to be there to pick them up. For the others, you've gotta sort out temporary accommodation. Someone has to go to the bank, then we're all in the office stuffing cash into envelopes, so we can give people four hundred dollars to tide them over for the first few weeks.

Then it's a dash to the airport to meet the planes as they come into this special charter area in the domestic terminal, opposite a carwash, a KFC and the Krispy Kreme donuts. People everywhere, excited, confused. Frazzled Red Cross workers running around, shouting instructions down their mobiles to an interpreting service …

We would hand over the envelopes of money in the carwash car park, one by one, getting them to count out it all out—one, two, three times—then sign for it. We were always doing this in the dark, sometimes it was raining, always windy … One night, while we were waiting for a plane with about seventy people coming in, I was put in charge of the cash. I'm walking around a carwash with about thirty thousand dollars in a fucking ALDI bag.

Bringing an asylum seeker off the plane to be reunited with family—after years, sometimes decades of separation—was one of the best parts of the job. For the other asylum seekers, we'd take them either to a Formule One motel or the Ibis. They could have a room for six weeks before they had to have found their own accommodation. We used the Ibis on the Princes Highway in St Peters a lot—

AUNTY RHONDA: The one that's down the road from the IKEA store?

KATIE: Yeah, that's it. There would be times when up to one hundred asylum seekers were staying in there. We were great for business.

THE LAWYER AND HIS REFUGEE CLIENTS: PART TWO

KAZ *resumes their 'headphone verbatim' rendition of words originally spoken by their friend, the lawyer Joe Tan.*

KAZ/JOE: You know there were other things, let's be honest, you know, there were other things driving me in that case ...

We amended the claim half-way through to basically, umm, involve a, umm, a false imprisonment claim, that they were, ah, in detention unlawfully ...

What it would have meant, if there was a finding by a court against the government, if this thing were to go to trial, was that every single person who had been detained on PNG, on Manus, and on Nauru had been illegally detained. And they would—they would basically have been—the government would have been up for millions and millions of dollars in compensation to every single person who was detained from 2001 onwards. It was massive!

And I wanted to be the one; to be the lawyer that got that case to the High Court and basically destroy the Pacific Solution ...

But for various reasons I moved out of that, ah, that particular department to somewhere else in Legal Aid and I had to give up the case. I tried everything to hold onto it ... but eventually ... I had to leave ... It went to someone else ... and I think it was settled because Legal Aid just didn't want it to go anywhere near a hearing, umm, because ... we were basically biting the hand that feeds us. The government is paying our wages and paying the budget to run this case against itself.

And they were preparing to make big cuts to Legal Aid and it was just a very sensitive time ... What I heard anecdotally ... was that it settled for a much, much lower amount than it should have. So, umm, and I wasn't involved to see the thing to the end but I would have pushed it much harder.

SCULPTURES BY THE SEA

KATIE *and* MAHDI *stand and tell this story together, partly addressing each other and partly editorialising for the audience.*

KATIE: One stinking hot day we organised a trip to 'Sculptures by the Sea' at Bondi. I think there were about fifty of us, five or six staff from Red Cross and the rest were asylum seekers who had only been in the community for a couple of weeks. So, we all piled onto the three-eighty bus ...

MAHDI: The three-eighty bus ... There was this caseworker standing up the back. She was a little bit different. The other caseworkers were just talking to each other, but she was talking to all of us, telling us that we were going to see some art. And I said 'Hey, I'm an artist from Afghanistan. I make theatre for women's rights'.

KATIE: 'Are you serious?' I'd met lots of interesting asylum seekers—they've all got amazing stories—but a feminist theatre-maker from Kabul!?!

MAHDI: Ha ha wow. A feminist theatre maker!

KATIE: My word, not his.

MAHDI: Yeah, for a lot of people in Afghanistan, 'feminist' means you hate men or you're a lesbian. But when she explained to me, I said 'yeah, I guess I am a feminist theatre director'.

MAHDI's photo from the outing to 'Sculptures by the Sea' comes up on screen.

KATIE: So here we are at Tamarama. It was so hot. It was really crowded. All our clients wanted us to take photos with them. I was worried that we were going to lose someone, that someone might drown.

MAHDI: There were a lot of things around. Piles of wood, old things, mattresses and stuff. I was wondering, 'Where is this art that they are talking about?' I didn't know that everything around me was actually the art. I thought it was just where people were throwing their junk!

KATIE: Sculptures by the Sea! One of the sculptures was this woman, larger than life, striking a yoga pose ...

MAHDI: Yeah, like this. We were trying to copy it.

KATIE: And this guy ...

MAHDI: Was he a tourist?

KATIE: I don't know. Some dickhead basically goes to, like, to pretend to eat out this woman's vagina and get his friend to take a photo. But you guys were like so fucking horrified and we're like, 'We're so sorry, and that man's disgusting.' The way you guys reacted was so—it was sweet, really, cause this guy was just an idiot.

MAHDI: Yeah, I was thinking 'This is freedom? This is what you do with your freedom?'

KATIE: These guys have only been out of detention a couple of weeks. This is their first engagement with public art and the Australian public in all our glory!

MAHDI: Yeah. But that broken boat ...

KATIE: Yeah.

MAHDI: Everyone was, ah ... Everyone had something with that broken boat.

KATIE: It was just a sculpture.

MAHDI: We came in the same boat—something like this wooden fishing boat, but this looks better. I was like ... because it was just two, three months that we were released, and everyone had a flashback. That wasn't a good thing for us ...

KATIE: There was this real rush of people telling me their boat stories— how scared they were; how the engine broke; how they ran out of water on the first day; how many days before the Navy arrived; how people drowned around them; how their boat smashed on the rocks; how they drifted at sea; how they tried to sleep so if the boat sank, they would die in their sleep ...

Segue into ...

END OF IMMIGRATION INTERVIEW / MAHDI LOVES TO DANCE

PAUL/IMMIGRATION OFFICER: After your arrival you were advised that the Australian Government has implemented new laws for asylum seekers arriving by boat on or after Thirteenth August 2012. This means you may be sent to a regional processing centre outside Australia where your claims will be assessed—currently these locations are Nauru and Manus Island, Papua New Guinea. Do you understand what that means?

> JAWAD, *in Hazaragi, tells* MAHDI *what to say ('Farad bego.'* *'Yes.')*

MAHDI: Yes.

PAUL/IMMIGRATION OFFICER: Is there any reason why you cannot be taken to a regional processing country, such as Nauru and Manus Island, Papua New Guinea?

> JAWAD, *in Hazaragi, tells* MAHDI *what to say ('Farad bego.' 'No.')*

MAHDI: No.

PAUL/IMMIGRATION OFFICER: Do you wish to be considered for voluntary return to your home country?

> JAWAD, *in Hazaragi, tells* MAHDI *what to say ('Farad bego.' 'No.')*

MAHDI: No.

PAUL/IMMIGRATION OFFICER: Why did you choose Australia as your destination?

MAHDI: Because I heard it is a country where you can be free. Where people have rights.

PAUL/IMMIGRATION OFFICER: Is there anything I have not asked you that you would like to say?

MAHDI: Yes ... Sometimes, boys and girls in Afghanistan, we make a party. It's very dangerous. If you get caught, you can get into a lot of trouble. But we love to dance.

> MAHDI *starts to make small dance movements ... Afghan dance party music fades in ... his movements become more energetic as it builds ... He leads all the cast (bar* PAUL*) in a joyous dance interlude ...*

INTRODUCING THE CODE OF BEHAVIOUR

PAUL *weaves his way through the dancing cast members and signals to the sound desk for the music to be cut.* KATIE, KAZ *and* JAWAD *leave the stage.* AUNTY RHONDA *and* MAHDI *stay. Paul shoves a document in* MAHDI'*s face before sharing its contents with the audience.*

PAUL: 'Department of Immigration and Border Protection, Code of Behaviour for asylum seekers who have been released into the community on a bridging visa.

'If you are found to have breached the Code of Behaviour [...] your visa may be cancelled. If your visa is cancelled, you will be returned to immigration detention and may be transferred to an offshore processing centre.

'While you are living in the Australian community:

'You must not disobey any Australian laws, including Australian road laws.'

You've got a car, Mahdi? Yeah? You ever drive over the speed limit? You ever gone through a red light? No? Good. Keep it that way.

'You must not make sexual contact with another person without that person's consent, regardless of their age ...

'You must not take part in or get involved in any kind of criminal behaviour in Australia, including violence against any person, including your family or government officials ...

'You must not harass, intimidate or bully any other person or group of people. You must not engage in any anti-social or disruptive activities that are inconsiderate, disrespectful or threaten the peaceful enjoyment of other members of the community.'

AUNTY RHONDA *has heard enough. She crosses the stage to confront* PAUL *who exits hastily, leaving the stage to* MAHDI *and* AUNTY RHONDA.

AUNTY RHONDA AND MAHDI SHARE STORIES

AUNTY RHONDA: I know what a Code of Behaviour is. I grew up under the racist *Aboriginal Protection Act*. They stopped us from speaking our language, dancing our dances, accessing our spiritual areas. They took the fairer skinned children away and put them into institutions. A lot of grief and sadness came from that. It carries on to this day.

I'm homeless at the moment, I'm couch surfing and I am sixty-five years old. I am a grandmother of ten. My uncle is a Senior Law Man, and he has acknowledged me as an Elder. And I was greatly honoured to be acknowledged in that way from a Senior Law Man.

Mahdi, I want you to help me with this cloak ...

He helps AUNTY RHONDA *turn the possum skin cloak inside out, allowing the audience to see the outlines of some images that have been burnt into the underside of the possum skin pelts with an engraving tool.* AUNTY RHONDA *points to these images as she talks.*

These are my totems. Umburra, the black duck, is my Yuin totem. And the possum is my Darug totem.

When the cloak was being made there was a process. A smoking ceremony was performed by Yuin Senior Law Man Uncle Max Dulumunmun Harrison to cleanse and bless the cloak.

The artwork was discussed—what was to go on the cloak, what symbols of cultural and spiritual importance to strengthen and give power, peace and love for the truth-telling and the healing.

So, I'm sharing some of my story with you now …

During the following stories, some images from AUNTY RHONDA*'s family photo albums are projected on an upstage screen or on the back wall of the theatre.*

I was born in Sydney in 1951 and grew up around Waterloo and Erskineville. My traditional people are the Darug from Sydney area, the Gadigal, the Bidjigal/Dharawal, the whale dreamers from La Perouse, and the Yuin people from the far South Coast.

My father, Charles 'Chicka' Dixon, lived on Wallaga Lake and La Perouse missions, with all my extended family. I remember I had to write to the mission manager for permission if I wanted to visit family or friends. Their lives were so controlled. Dad's father and his two brothers were taken from their parents and put into Kinchela Boys Home. They were treated very cruel in there.

I was mostly brought up by my mum's parents. Nanna was sent out from the mission to clean the white people's houses on the North Shore. We never crossed the bridge, but I remember her being really fanatical about cleaning and polishing at home because we'd get visits from the Welfare, unannounced. They'd have the white gloves on; they'd run their finger along the sideboard or the shelves, looking for dust; they'd check your kitchen cupboards to see what food you had. But Nanna knew how to keep house like a good white person, so the Welfare didn't take us.

I remember when I was little, I used to go out to 'Lapa' [La Perouse] and see my Dad there. He lived in a little tin shack. He was a full-on alcoholic at that time. But when I was about ten, he straightened himself out and became a full-on activist. He said: 'While ever I fight for my people, I will never, ever drink.' And he was true to that. He was involved in setting up the Aboriginal Tent Embassy, the Aboriginal Medical Service and Aboriginal Legal Service. I grew up going to all these demonstrations with my Dad.

But we are still trying to psychologically heal from the trauma that's been passed down through the generations. The 'gap' isn't closing—we are three per cent of the total population but forty-eight per cent of young people who are incarcerated in this country are Aboriginal. In Western Australia, it goes up to eighty per cent. In the Northern Territory, ninety-seven per cent. Our young people are killing themselves—suicide is the leading cause of death for young Aboriginal people. Every Aboriginal person is touched by these deaths. I deal with this stuff all the time. When is this gonna stop? When is this ever gonna stop? It's gotta stop.

MAHDI glances up at a photo of AUNTY RHONDA's granddad which has appeared on the screen ...

MAHDI: Aunty Rhonda, who's the singer?

AUNTY RHONDA: That's my granddad. He loved to entertain. Always singing, a bit of a dancer ...

MAHDI: Like me?

AUNTY RHONDA: Yeah. When he was gonna perform, granddad used to say: 'Don't be shy! You gotta put the go on!'

MAHDI: You gotta put the go on!

AUNTY RHONDA: That's it: 'You gotta put the go on. A bit of razzamataz.' He used to speak in language but because he grew up under the *Aboriginal Protection Act*, he didn't speak it around us, he didn't want us getting into any trouble.

MAHDI: I see ... One time, I was on the train with my cousin, we were talking in Hazaragi, our own language, and this lady—she leans over, taps me on the shoulder and says: 'You're in Australia! Do you mind speaking English!' I was straight away thinking of the Code of Behaviour. I can't say anything.

He sits down with AUNTY RHONDA.

I have a friend who doesn't want to wear Afghan clothes in case people think he's a terrorist. He came home one day and he said:

'The way that you sit—it's Afghan. Aussies sit like this.' So, after that, we sit like this. When I walk around, I look at the ground most of the time. I don't want to make any trouble. I don't want to engage with people. I don't want to make people get angry at me.

One day, in our flat, we were having a party. The music was a bit loud, but it was during the day. And then this neighbour, an Australian man, came to us, banged on the door and said: 'Turn off the music! Otherwise, I will call the police!' And my friend just freaked out. He took the stereo and threw it out of the window. And he said: 'After now, no more music, no more parties in this house'. Because he was afraid to be sent back into detention.

An aerial photo of Scherger Detention Centre comes up.

That's Scherger Detention Centre. My room was in this hut. And you see that tree? That's where I used to sit every night, thinking about my past, thinking about my future.

There was this woman—one of the guards—she was nice. She asked me to sit with her once and she was asking 'What did you used to do in Afghanistan?' I said I was a director of theatre and cinema. She said, 'What is theatre?'

AUNTY RHONDA: What's theatre?!

> AUNTY RHONDA *laughs, picks up a ukulele, and starts strumming.*

MAHDI: I said 'Oh, it's like a show, performing … ' Then she understood my meaning, but she said 'Oh, that's not a good job. In Australia, a good job is like engineering or construction worker.' But I want to keep making theatre.

AUNTY RHONDA: Hey Mahdi, listen to this …

> AUNTY RHONDA *sings a stirring rendition of 'Miss Celie's Blues', with finger-clicking accompaniment from* MAHDI *and a little tap dance from* KATIE *who re-enters the stage during the song's chorus.*
>
> AUNTY RHONDA *takes a round of applause and* MAHDI *escorts her back to her 'Convenor's seat'.*

I used to sing that while my daughter played the guitar, but I thought I'd teach myself to play it on the ukelele.

> MAHDI *is about to exit but turns back to address* AUNTY RHONDA.

MAHDI: Aunty Rhonda ... Some of our young people are killing themselves too. While we have been making this show, there's been four suicides of people I know.

MAHDI *exits.*

FREQUENTLY ASKED QUESTIONS

The text in this section is from a document that was distributed to doctors, nurses, and counsellors employed by the multinational company, International Medical and Health Services, under contract with the Australian Government, to provide care for asylum seekers and refugees on Manus and Nauru. The document was circulated after the death of Reza Berati during a violent invasion of the Manus detention centre in 2014.

KATIE: [*speaking into a hand-held microphone*] 'We understand that you feel unsafe after all that has happened. It will take a while to feel safe again and we are all working to make that happen. Come and see us if you find that you are frightened all the time. We are here to help you as best we can.'

PAUL *enters, takes the mic from* KATIE *who moves into position for the movement sequence that is to follow.*

PAUL: 'All this happened in the dark in a very volatile situation. You could say that it was an awful accident but that would not adequately describe what you have been through. Sometimes bad things happen to good people and there is no reason.'

JAWAD *enters and takes the mic.*

JAWAD: 'If you are having nightmares, feeling very anxious or like you can't stop thinking about what has happened then please come to see us. We will talk things through and see what we can do to help.'

MAHDI *enters and takes the mic.*

MAHDI: 'We are sure that from your experience you understand that the people of a country are not the same as the government. There are many Australians who care and want to help.'

KAZ *enters and takes the mic.*

KAZ: 'If you have survived war or other bad situations, you can survive this. You have tremendous strength and resilience. Manus is a tough place, so you have to eat well, and exercise and keep your brain working. These are the things you must do to keep strong.'

'DARK TECHNO' MOVEMENT INTERLUDE

As KAZ *finishes their text, a 'dark techno' soundtrack starts to build.* KATIE, PAUL, JAWAD, MAHDI *and* KAZ *perform a nightmarish movement sequence that cites some of their gestures from earlier in the show.*

The sequence comes to a halt as AUNTY RHONDA *moves among the performers and gently directs their attention to the arrival of some guests.*

The soundtrack fades and a warmer lighting state is established.

A TEA BREAK

As the 'Dark Techno' sequence is ending, guests have quietly arrived on stage with urns, crockery, tea pots, sweets, and biscuits. At many performances in Sydney, these guests would be representatives from The Parents' Café, an organisation based in Fairfield that runs a community garden, provides catering for special events, and offers vocational training in hospitality for recently arrived migrants and refugees. At other performances, it might be friends of MAHDI *and* JAWAD *from the local Afghan community.*

AUNTY RHONDA: Tea is served.

> *The performers have withdrawn from the 'dark techno' choreography, accepted cups of tea, and sat themselves down on the stage. Members of the audience are also offered tea and biscuits.*

Thank you. The tea is lovely. The biscuits are very nice too. Well, members of the audience, as the convenor of the People's Tribunal, I would really like to hear from the people. Kaz, could you facilitate, please?

KAZ: Yes, Aunty Rhonda.

A SPACE FOR CONVERSATION

Partly inspired by Lois Weaver's 'Long Table' events, the idea for the following section is described by Kaz Therese as 'creating a potential collapse of the show or of the structures of theatre'. The aim is to allow the room to become uncomfortable for a moment (despite the tea and biscuits on offer), so that the audience is not exactly sure what's happening and a space for subtle subversion can be opened; where the dramatic structure is in tension with the pressing real time concerns and 'real life' emotional conflicts and complexities of the lives and themes explored in the show. In practice, this section of the show would run for 15–20 minutes. There would be an initial guest speaker, time for audience members to contribute to the conversation if they wished, and then a closing contribution, usually by artists from the Bankstown Poetry Slam community.

KAZ: So, to begin the conversation, I see [*insert name of guest speaker*] is in the audience with us tonight. Would you like to come down and join us onstage?

GUEST SPEAKER #1

A guest speaker is introduced to the audience to speak about their experience of refugee resettlement issues. Speakers have included the staff of local NGOs created by refugees for the support of refugees, refugee advocates involved with Amnesty International and other groups, and a psychotherapist, specialising in trauma-informed counselling.

AUDIENCE CONTRIBUTIONS

After the guest speaker has helped break the ice, KAZ *opens up the conversation to contributions from the audience. There are usually at least three or four audience members willing to comment on what they have seen and heard in the performance, or else seeking more advice about how to welcome refugees, what political actions might best support their human rights, et cetera.*

KAZ: Would anyone like to ask a question to [*insert name of guest speaker*] or to anyone on the Tribunal? Or make a statement?

> KAZ *and the rest of the cast quietly sip their tea and scan the audience. It is fine for there to be a long, deep, heavy silence. We reproduce here a small sample of audience contributions, as recorded on the archival video documentation of the original production of* Tribunal *at Griffin Theatre:*

AUDIENCE MEMBER #1: Yep.

KAZ: Hi.

AUDIENCE MEMBER #1: Why do you think some Australians agree with the 'Pacific Solution'?

> KAZ *looks around to see who, from the* Tribunal *cast, might want to respond.* MAHDI *laughs and indicates that it's not really his place to say, given the chilling effect of the 'Code of Behaviour' on criticism by TPV holders of the government or of Australian citizens.*

AUDIENCE MEMBER #2: [*subsequently identified as Alison Lyssa, a Sydney-based playwright*] Can I answer it?

PAUL: Go for it.

AUDIENCE MEMBER #2/ALISON LYSSA: From my point of view, not from anyone else's point of view … My dad was a boat person in 1926, when he was sixteen years old, but he was a boat person from England. I was on a train, travelling to my privileged position as a teacher at the university, and I was sitting in that part of the train where you can sit and converse with your fellow passengers, the little vestibule before you go up or down the stairs, and the ticket collectors came through. And I was sharing that vestibule with people whose face is like the faces of the people here—

> *She gestures towards the Afghan performers on stage.*

I was the only one with a face that had come from England. And I was the only one that the ticket collectors didn't want to see my ticket! So, I leapt to my feet—

> *She jumps up out of her seat.*

—and I shouted: 'Come back!'

TRIBUNAL

The cast and other audience members laugh and applaud. She sits back down.

GUEST PERFORMERS

The open conversation with the audience culminates in a guest performance by members of the Bankstown Poetry Slam community. There is a moment of subterfuge here—as if these perfomers just happen to be in the audience and have been moved to want to contribute something special—but, of course, audience members soon realise, and warm to, the fact that this is a planned moment of 'performance exchange'.

AUNTY RHONDA CLOSES THE 'FORMAL' PROCEEDINGS

After the final guest speakers/performers have completed their presentations, AUNTY RHONDA *makes a final statement to the audience.*

AUNTY RHONDA: Thank you very much. Thank you, everyone, for your contributions. Please feel free to hang around in the foyer if there's more questions you'd like to ask or stories to share. Tell your friends that the Tribunal is still in session (*'for the rest of this week'* ... *or insert relevant days*).

What will it take for we—the people—to bring our representatives to the point where they are willing to hear the truth and repair the damage they have done to so many? Let us just take a moment to think about this ...

CODA: 'THERE WERE THREE YOUNG MEN ... '

After a suitable moment of silence, JAWAD *stands and starts talking to* MAHDI *in Hazaragi, teasing him a little bit, telling him he needs to work out ... The following is a rough scaffold for their semi-improvised conversation in Hazaragi.*

JAWAD: Come on Mahdi. Let's do some exercise. You're getting soft. You've been in Australia too long.

They start warming up. Shoulder rolls, arm swings etc. JAWAD *is clear and focused.* MAHDI *less so.*

MAHDI: I'm working hard. I'm learning to become a bricklayer.

JAWAD: That's good. Next you will become a construction worker. Come on.

> JAWAD *leads* MAHDI *into touching toes and other stretches;* MAHDI *keeps looking for opportunities to catch his breath and shift the topic of conversation ... But* JAWAD *sees what is happening and keeps moving* MAHDI *onto another exercise ...*

MAHDI: You know, I think half of the houses in Western Sydney have been built by Afghan refugees.

JAWAD: Is this what you thought you would be doing when we were sharing that room in Indonesia?

MAHDI: We had some good times.

JAWAD: Yes, when I was doing the cooking.

MAHDI: Come on, you know that's not true. I am a really good cook. You liked the food I prepared.

JAWAD: Your cooking is a disaster but your dancing is okay. You could have stayed with me in Indonesia. I told you not to get on the boat, that it was better to wait and hope for the UN to send us as refugees to Australia.

MAHDI: I couldn't wait that long. I'm not going to waste three years of my life doing nothing.

JAWAD: I was doing things. I learned Indonesian. I taught myself English.

MAHDI: Yes, but I want to keep being an artist, to make theatre.

JAWAD: So? I've only been here two months and now I am in this play. I didn't even go to the Fine Arts Faculty in Kabul to study theatre. I never finished high school. I think my English is better than yours. That's why they gave me the role of translator.

MAHDI: Okay, shut up. You know you are only here because of me.

> *They share a laugh.*

MAHDI: [*switching to English*] Have you heard from Nabi?

JAWAD: [*replying in English*] Nabi ... Okay, let's talk about Nabi.

> JAWAD *addresses the audience. Both performers switch to English for the following lines.*

There were three young men. Sharing a tiny room in a boarding house. On the edge of the city of Bogor. In Indonesia. They met there for the first time. They became good friends. They are all Afghan asylum seekers.

> *Image comes up on screen of* MAHDI, JAWAD, *and their friend Nabi ...* JAWAD *points to* MAHDI.

Mahdi left. His boat sank but he made it to Australia.

MAHDI: [*pointing to* JAWAD] Jawad stayed ...

JAWAD: I was thinking about the boat, but I thought it was too risky. And now I am one of the very lucky ones—it's just chance—I was picked to come to Australia under the UN refugee resettlement program. I arrived by plane.

> JAWAD *points upstage to a projected photograph of their friend, Nabi.*

And Nabi ... He took a boat just after Mahdi but he was too late ... He is on Manus Island now. He has been there since 2013. Sometimes we share messages on Facebook. The last time I was talking to him on the phone, he was telling me the conditions are really terrible, then he said 'Sorry, I have to go now'. I asked him why, but he just said the guard was coming and they don't like you to talk ... I think it is very hard for him. And he has done nothing wrong. He is the same as us.

MAHDI: So, this is a song for Nabi ...

> MAHDI *explains in Hazaragi to* JAWAD: *'Just listen and follow me ... I'll teach you.'*
>
> MAHDI *leads* JAWAD *in the singing of a song about friends who have travelled over the seas in search of a better life. The song is sung in Dari. An English translation of the song lyrics could be projected on the upstage screen/walls:*
>
> This is everything that is.
> Good or bad,
> This is the world.
> This is how it is.
> Separation is a lonely death.

A paradise on the other side
Of the ocean
Is just a promise.
This side of the ocean is the same
As the other side of the ocean.

Fade to black.

THE END

ASYLUM FESTIVAL

*A festival curated and produced by
Apocalypse Theatre Company*

Introduction

Festivals have played an important role in the production and reception of refugee-related theatre in Australia. For example, the Sydney Festival premiered the verbatim play *Through the Wire* as a work-in-progress in 2004, while the Melbourne Festival's season of Théâtre du Soleil's *Le Dernier Caravansérail* sold out in 2005. While these festivals tried to bring refugee-related performance to mainstream audiences, resettlement services often stage festivals within and for migrant communities. For instance, since 2015, Sydney's Settlement Services International has staged their New Beginnings Festival. Then there are festivals like Apocalypse Theatre Company's *ASYLUM*, which was staged in February 2015 in a small theatre in inner Sydney. Instead of targeting the mainstream or a particular migrant community, this festival addressed an audience who could be described as concerned, interested, activated and even activist, or, as one broadcaster noted in that great pejorative term, 'the converted' (Cathcart 2015).

The *ASYLUM* festival came about when Apocalypse issued an open call inviting playwrights from across Australia to respond to the theme of what it means to seek asylum. It asked, 'How will our stage respond to Operation Sovereign Borders? What do our great storytellers have to say?' ('Asylum' n.d.). Though the call was open for only a month, the company received 40 proposals (Blake 2015). Twenty-four writers were then given 15 days to deliver the final script. The works were rehearsed with actors and directors over a single weekend and then performed as staged readings over 12 nights across two weeks at the Old 505 Theatre in Surry Hills.

Quick-response initiatives usually revolve around public snap actions, such as protests or digital interventions like RISE's 'we will not be silenced' (2016). Theatre, by contrast, often has a long lead time, and the journey from conception to production can sometimes take years. In compressing the process to just a few months, *ASYLUM* bridged activism with stage theatre. As Apocalypse's founder and artistic director, Dino Dimitriadis, described it, *ASYLUM* was 'an experiment in quick response theatre that allows writers to take a snapshot of our time' (Blake 2015). In undertaking this experiment, Dimitriadis asserted that artists are important contributors to the conversation about border policies, border experiences and border violence. While there was a risk that 'some of the material might be outdated in a month', the other, more likely risk is that it would remain depressingly relevant for years—as the publication of these scripts in 2023 attests (Blake 2015). Regardless, the rapid response format brought more voices, more swiftly to the Australian stage.

Beyond speed, the project also sought nuance and variety. The selection panel for *ASYLUM* looked for breadth and deleted buzzwords such as 'queue jumpers' to have a conversation that, though working with immediate headlines, aspired to find ways beyond them as well. 'We tried to find stories that were ... localised and personal to strike at the universal', said Dimitriadis ('Asylum Seekers' Chronicles on Stage' 2015). The season included a range of lengths and styles—from naturalistic plays to verbatim theatre, monologues, absurdist works, poetry and puppetry. They were grouped into five programs, with four to six works in each, making 29 plays in total. In addition to diverse forms, *ASYLUM* also sought diverse voices, programming a mixture of new, emerging and established playwrights. There were also writers who identified as asylum seekers or refugees at the time of submitting their works. In the performance space, there hung art works by visual artist and asylum seeker Fakhrudin Rajai. In addition to the 24 writers, 10 directors, 32 actors and 10 crew helped to stage the *ASYLUM* festival.

It is impossible to represent the entire festival within this volume, so we have chosen three plays to represent it: Noëlle Janaczewska's *Going for Gold*, Tania Cañas' *Three Angry Australians* and Georgia Symons' *A Puppet Show for All Ages*. Together, these three plays speak to the range of voices, forms and tones that emerged as well as the surprising prominence of comedy, a genre that was not so common in theatrical responses to the Pacific Solution (Wake 2015). The scene is set in Janaczewska's *Going for Gold*, where 'Team Australia'—a phrase borrowed from former prime minister Tony Abbott—is competing in an imaginary Olympics of Cruelty. According to the play, the Americans might dominate 'Waterboarding', but the Australians are hot favourites for the 'Punishing Asylum Seekers' event. Cañas' *Three Angry Australians* is set in an NGO office during a typical day's work as a pro-refugee protest occurs just outside. The characters chat between themselves as they manage obtrusive phone calls and extractive emails. The piece questions what resistance is and what it looks like, particularly from those who have directly experienced border violence. It also reads as a companion piece to her influential essay '10 Things You Need to Consider If You Are an Artist Not of the Refugee and Asylum Seeker Community Looking to Work with Our Community' (Cañas 2015). Finally, Symon's monologue *A Puppet Show for All Ages* explores the parallels between the stage and reality with the character of Zeinah finding herself in the body of the Actor. There is an initial struggle, then jubilation, as the character notes she can do what she likes, including cartwheels, and tries to explain what happened to her own body to the audience, who believe her.

In both its process and outcome, *ASYLUM* made a unique contribution to refugee theatre in Australia, offering a platform for various voices to speak rapidly and directly to the shifting political dynamics. For this reason, Apocalypse did not seek finished, resolved or highly polished works, instead centring content and engaging the audience in a timely, urgent conversation. Finally, it is worth noting that all the creatives involved worked for free, and all proceeds were donated to the Asylum Seeker Resource Centre in Melbourne and the Asylum Seeker Centre in Sydney. 'It really is a community project', said Dimitriadis ('Australian Playwrights Confront One of the Country's Greatest Social and Political Problems' 2015).

References

'Asylum'. n.d. *Apocalypse Theatre*. https://www.apocalypsetheatre.com.au/asylum.

'Asylum Seekers' Chronicles on Stage'. 2015. *Point Magazine*, 15 February. http://www.thepointmagazine.com.au/post.php?s=2015-02-16-asylum-seekers-chronicles-on-stage.

'Australian Playwrights Confront One of the Country's Greatest Social and Political Problems'. 2015. *Theatre People*, 30 January. https://web.archive.org/web/20210801065918/https://www.theatrepeople.com.au/australian-playwrights-confront-one-of-our-countrys-greatest-social-and-political-problems/.

Blake, Elissa. 2015. 'Asylum Plays Offer Rapid-Responses Theatre Treatment of Refugee Issue'. *Sydney Morning Herald*, 1 February. https://www.smh.com.au/entertainment/theatre/asylum-plays-offer-rapidresponse-theatre-treatment-of-refugee-issue-20150201-1331t2.html.

Cañas, Tania. 2015. 'Some Points To Consider If You're An Artist Who Wants To Make Work About Refugees'. E-flux Conversations, October. https://conversations.e-flux.com/t/some-points-to-consider-if-youre-an-artist-who-wants-to-make-work-about-refugees/2716.

Cathcart, Michael. 2015. 'Asylum: A Series of New Plays'. *ABC Radio National*, 2 February. https://www.abc.net.au/radionational/programs/archived/booksandarts/asylum3a-a-new-play/6061468.

RISE: Refugee Survivors and Ex-Detainees. 2016. 'First Nations Liberation, RISE & WAR Present : Sovereignty + Sanctuary : A First Nations / Refugee Solidarity Event.' 15 June. https://www.riserefugee.org/sovereignty-sanctuary/.

Wake, Caroline. 2015. 'Voicing Empathy, Rehearsing Protest: Apocalypse Theatre, *Asylum*'. *RealTime* 126 (April–May): 4–5. https://www.realtime.org.au/voicing-empathy-rehearsing-protest/.

GOING FOR GOLD

Noelle Janaczewska

Chris Fung in Apocalypse Theatre Company's Going for Gold, *2015 (Photo: Robert Catto)*

Going for Gold was first produced by Apocalypse Theatre Company in 2015 as part of the *ASYLUM* Festival show at The Old 505 Theatre in Sydney.

    PERFORMERS   Chris Fung
                                            Courtney Stewart-Smith
                                            Kirsty Marillier
                                            Michael Wood

Director, Michelle Miall

It was adapted to form part of Australian Performance Exchange's *Origin–Transit–Destination* also in 2015.

NOTE

Going for Gold is written for a chorus, a speaking choir of voices. A team of at least three, preferably more. It also lends itself to a large cast production.

A — at the beginning of a line indicates a change of speaker.

Lines in **bold** are spoken by more than one performer. Lines can overlap or be repeated.

Random whistles, cheers, applause and shots from (starters') pistols punctuate the piece.

Around everyone's neck is a medal.

They all step onto a podium/into the glare of a post-event press conference.

As they field questions and recount their journey to gold-medal glory, they wave and make gestures of victory.

— Today's victory represents a lot of hard work, by a lot of people.
— Let's recap for those at home.
— It was a wide open field and the title was up for grabs.
— There were obvious favourites.
— We knew we were front-runners.
— But we didn't underestimate the competition.
— It was a close call.
— We were over the moon when the committee made Punishing Asylum Seekers an international sport. We knew they'd added Waterboarding, and of course the Americans dominate that event. But Punishing Asylum Seekers—that's where Australia really punches above its weight. We were a shoo-in for a medal, but more than that, we were determined to
— **Go for gold!**
— Our treatment of asylum seekers was already draconian. If we lifted our game we could make it even harsher.
— **Go for gold!**
— If we don't let the wussies and bleeding hearts stuff up our pitch, it could be
— **Aussie, Aussie, Aussie!**
  Gold, gold, gold!
— People say it's easy, but it isn't. The Luge is easy: flat on your back on a sledge and it's downhill all the way. Punishing Asylum Seekers needs a particular mindset, tunnel vision, and buckets of money.
— What we brought to the competition wasn't only our past experience—
— Like the White Australia policy.
— But also our willingness to try completely new tactics—

— Delete bits of the country from the national map. Offshore detention. Skip human rights. Bribe cash-strapped countries to take our unwashed refugees …

Awkward pause.

The speaker explains.

— Uh, yeah, no, sorry. I misspoke there, slip of the tongue. I mean our unwanted refugees.
— **Unwanted.**
— We sailed though the heats, no sweat. Lebanon, Jordan, Pakistan, Canada, Italy—never in the running. In the semis we knocked out Denmark, Japan and the UK. Then came the final and we were bracing for a real contest.
— Our motto:
— **Australia—harder to get into than North Korea.**
— Naturally there have been injuries along the way.
— And deaths. But none of them serious.
— The mistake we made before was bringing asylum seekers to the mainland and basically looking after them while their claims were processed.
— So we came up with a new game plan.
— It wasn't easy. Equestrian sports are easy. You get to sit down and the horse does it all for you. This wasn't easy.
— Well, yeah, there was opposition out there in the community. But we kept our heads down and ignored it.
— We had our strategy, and we stuck with it.
— On track!
— Eyes on the prize!
— Eyes on the finish line, and asylum seekers out of sight.
— **Out of sight. Out of reach. Out of touch.**
— Yes, of course I remember before, when we liked refugees and provided them with milk bars and market gardens. And yes, the garlic and zucchini years were good years. And after that we had the pork roll years, and they were okay as well. But it's a whole different ball game now. The rules are much tougher and there are way more penalties.
— Look. If you want a chance in this competition, you've gotta play to win. It's an endurance sport, and that means pushing the limits …

— This is a massive win for Team Australia. We started with Stop the Boats. And that wasn't easy. Rowing is easy. Well, maybe not for the athletes who do the hard yakka with the oars, but for the guy who sits at the end and yells at them—piece of cake.
— Australia has invested big time in training their team, getting them up to speed for this event. And it shows.
— As they race towards the line, the crowd is cheering—Yes! Team Australia's going to take the gold!
— And Wow! Yes! It's gold and glory all the way for Australia!
— **Gold and glory!**
— We played to win, and we did.
— We won!

Lots of rah-rah and jumping up and down and cheering.

— Once we signed a deal with Cambodia to take asylum seekers off our hands, we knew we were in pole position. Sure the Americans have those gun-toting vigilantes on the Mexican border, but we had pretty much our whole government—not to mention the opposition—going in to bat for us.
— It all happened so fast.
— It might look easy on TV, but it isn't.
— Indoor Volleyball is easy if you want to avoid accountability. You've got five teammates to toss around the blame. Plus who really gives a shit about Indoor Volleyball? Whereas popular, high-profile sports like Punishing Asylum Seekers, we've got a responsibility. We've got a lot of people's hopes and dreams riding on us.
— I'm not going to comment on the tears. Crocodile tears, they said in the media, and that's good enough for me.
— There's always controversy at any sporting event. Always some meltdown. People are on edge, emotions running high.
— And it's pure gold! Australia has smashed the record for Punishing Asylum Seekers! Australia has lifted this sport to a whole new level! Australia is the undisputed world champion!

More rah-rah and jumping up and down and cheering.

The performers kiss their medals.

— If history repeats itself, I think we can expect the same thing again.

— Team Australia's crafty tactics have really put Punishing Asylum Seekers on the sporting calendar. What's the betting other countries copy us in future competitions?
— Let's hear it for the winner.
— And the winner is—

Silence.

No one moves.

THE END

THREE ANGRY AUSTRALIANS

Tania Canas

Felino Dolloso, Jennifer Rani Gardner and Emily Havea in Apocalypse Theatre Company's THREE ANGRY AUSTRALIANS, 2015 (Photo: Robert Catto)

Three Angry Australians was first produced by Apocalypse Theatre Company as part of the *ASYLUM* Festival at The Old 505 Theatre in Sydney. It opened on 6 February 2015, with the following creative team:

PERFORMERS	Jennifer Rani Gardner
	Emily Havea
	Felino Dolloso

Director, Charlotte Bradley

Artist's Statement

I wrote in *Performing Exile: Foreign Bodies*, 'As a playwright, I wanted to use the opportunity to stage a different type of narrative, one that challenged the expectations I had directly encountered regarding the idea of a definitive, universal refugee narrative'(Cañas 2017, 63). *Three Angry Australians* was set at an NGO office during a typical day's work. The synopsis read: 'What discussions happen after that phone gets put down and after that email is sent? This is the raw discourse—in all its rage, political incorrectness and resistance' (Asylum 2015). I wanted a dry, satirical approach—no screaming, no running or hyperventilating characters—but to bring to stage the mundane (yet not mundane) border dynamics playing out in the everyday. The piece looked to question the colonially imposed linear understandings between refugee and Australian. I pushed for the cast to be all people of colour. 'I desired to see characters on stage grappling with the nuanced ethical dilemmas, the mundane and the administrative minutiae, the contradictions and confusion of refugeeness' (63). I also wanted to open up questions around public and private, visible and non-visible forms of advocacy and the distribution of labour.

References

'Asylum.' 2015. *Apocalypse Theatre Company,* February 2015: https://www.apocalypsetheatre.com.au/asylum

Cañas, Tania. 2017. '*Three Angry Australians*: A Reflexive Approach'. In *Performing Exile: Foreign Bodies*, edited by Judith Rudakoff, 59–74. Bristol: Intellect. https://doi.org/10.2307/j.ctv9hj90p.7

In blackout: the sound of a protest taking place outside: 'Free Free the Refugees, Free Free the Refugees'. The sound builds to a roar, then suddenly stops. Lights up. An office. Three people are working at their computers.

ONE: 'Name of organisation', 'How many refugees does your organisation support?', 'Please tick, the ethnicity of your clients below—

TWO: I am writing to seek referral for our member, not client—

THREE: See attached, kind regards—

ONE: Tick, tick, tick, tick—

THREE: Level Three Williams Landing Street—

ONE: 'Please tick the suburbs your organisation covers' tick tick—

TWO: See attached details and respond to me as soon as you can, as a matter of urgency—

ONE: Tick tick, Australian business number eighty-five eighty-nine—

TWO: Send.

ONE: Save

THREE: Send

Beat. The sound of the protest begins again, quietly at first, but grows increasingly loud.

'Please see below a three-part photography workshop that has reserved a number of FREE places for refugees/asylum seekers in detention (particularly youth). If you could kindly share widely that would be much appreciated, and feel free to contact me with any queries.'

TWO: 'To whom it may concern, just following up on our member,' [*To others*] not client, 'you referred'—

ONE: 'Does your organisation have endorsement as deductable gift recipient under subdivision Thirty-BA of the Income Tax Assessment Act, provide details below'—

ONE: From who?

THREE: International Solidarity Network, Melbourne.

TWO: I'd be careful with the Solidarity Network doing this. I suspect they will use it to promote themselves.

THREE: What do I respond?

ONE: Nothing.

TWO: Argh, what time did this thing start? You think it would be over by now?

ONE: Fortunately we don't have to reply.

THREE: One p.m., I think. You going later?

ONE: No, applying for the three-year organisational grant from Moss and Meg.

TWO: Who organised it? The socialists?

THREE: Not sure.

TWO: Let me see.

Looks up the information on the computer. Moment of silence.

Yep.

ALL: Arghhh.

ONE: The worst. I guess I'll just spend more time on this grant and get it done by today. This is my protest.

TWO: If there was a refugee organisation associated with it maybe, but not if it's just them. 'Free free the refugees', sounds so condescending when they say it like that.

ONE: Either way, I don't have the luxury of going out to the streets with a bunch of hipsters looking for a temporary cause.

TWO: Write grants, upskill our community, deliver a food pantry, keep up to date with developments on the issue. We go and study, work with community. Even getting a PhD is part of our political struggle This is the un-glamorous side of political activism. Noodles anyone?

Holds up a packet of two-minute noodles.

ONE / THREE: No thanks

THREE: So grateful to have this space. I can't talk like this out there.

ONE: If I join that protest; they'll probably look at my sneakers and assume I've sold out. It's okay for them in ripped shirts and dreads. Just cause I dress up doesn't mean I'm not struggling or working for the cause. As people of colour and refugees—we navigate differently. White people just don't know how to read it. They think it looks like that—

Points outside.

THREE: After my master's research talk regarding the expected staging, narrative and aesthetics of the refugee community, a white guy came up to me, looked me up and down and said 'you don't look like you struggle'.
ONE: Did you punch him in the face?

    TWO *continues to talk from kitchen.*

TWO: People like to demonstrate to demonstrate support but care is useless and in some cases even counterproductive. Care can mean anything and nothing. Like sympathy—what am I supposed to do with your sympathy? I'd prefer resonance.
ONE: Ppff.
TWO: Well, the hardest working people I know in this industry are not at this protest.
ONE: Nor do they win 'multicultural awards' or ambassadorships. Congratulations for being brown. Here is an award—look what an accepting nation we are. Our protest is in the work we do.
THREE: What if these people have good intentions? Don't work in the field and have no way to show it?
ONE: Pppft. Anyone can have good intentions. Some people really need to stop having good intentions.
THREE: So to protest, you have to completely dedicate your life to that particular issue? Work or be part of community? Is that humanly possible? There are so many issues out there.
ONE: Better to choose one and do it well than to just hold a megaphone.
THREE: All social issues are connected though.
TWO: Doesn't mean one needs to feel they have to always say something for each—knowing privilege is knowing how much space you already take up. I'd be interested in seeing how many members of our community are at that protest though.
ONE: Our existence is a protest. To go to a protest like that (*points outside*) is to parade.
THREE: That's a bit harsh.
TWO: 'There are men who struggle for a day and they are good. There are men who struggle for a year and they are better.'
ONE: For some it's an afternoon, for others it's a lifestyle.
TWO: 'There are men who struggle many years, and they are better

still. But there are those who struggle all their lives: These are the indispensable ones.' Bertolt Brecht.

ONE: We should tweet that

THREE: [*writing tweet*] —'There are men ... '

ONE: Tick tick. It's important to share that change happens when things become a movement—from the community up. Not one-off deeds.

TWO: Oh no.

Others move closer.

[*Reading off computer*] 'I'm currently working on a photographic series. I'm looking for refugees living in Melbourne as their stories are an incredibly important point of view to portray within the series. I won the ten-thousand-dollar National Photographic Prize earlier this year. I will give the sitter a copy of the portrait to keep. Cheers.'

ALL *wince.*

THREE: And she called it ' a photo project to change Australia'.

ALL *wince again.*

TWO: What do we respond?

ONE: Nothing, we shouldn't have to waste our time.

TWO: We have to respond; otherwise they'll never understand why.

ONE: If they don't know now, we shouldn't have to waste our time explaining the frameworks of self-determination, capacity building and how her project to 'change Australia' is just reinforcing power dynamics.

TWO: They need to understand why though, that's part of our job?

ONE: We are overstretched as it is and don't need such stupid emails to waste our time. My responsibility is to the community we are working with, not responding to every hero wannabe, loud mouth occupier of power as it is. I'm not going to contribute to their CV and humanitarian cause for the month.

THREE: We have to respond something.

ONE: How about this? [*Typing*] 'We are sorry, we do not supply models for art projects.'

TWO: Send. We should have a policy for responding to emails.

ONE: We should.

THREE: I could write one?

ONE: Put it on the agenda for the next meeting.
TWO: Junk mail, junk mail, theatre project junk mail.
ONE: 'Please attach your insurance certificate, notice of endorsement for charity tax concessions and last year's financial report.'
THREE: The refugee issue must be in vogue again, because there are a few emails coming through. 'I'm a documentary photographer from Cairns, Queensland. I'm currently working on a photographic exhibition which looks at the life of refugees in Australia—but through their eyes. And was wondering if you would be interested in being involved?'
TWO: Noo stop.
THREE: 'The idea first started about a year ago when I realised that one of the main things blocking Australians from essentially accepting asylum seekers in Australia was the media, the lack of personalisation … '
ONE: Oh cause we seek accepting and approval from you—what an enlightened individual you are. I suppose you will suggest that if we tell our personal stories that's how we will be accepted by welcoming Australia?
THREE: 'And I thought, if only Australians could see that Asylum seekers are just everyday people trying to survive, not crazy criminals trying to steal our land.' What?!
TWO: [*takes over reading*] 'From here the original idea was that I would spend a couple of months with different refugees—and take photos like "a day in the life in". But then I got a better idea … how much more powerful would this project be if the photos, the story was told by the refugee themselves?'
ONE: How did this guy make it all about him already?
THREE: 'From a practical side, the idea is this—To get in contact and find multiple different refugees. Ta.'
TWO: What an innovative idea.
ONE: Come and exhibit our individual faces and names. So that you can really understand that we are human. How sickening.
THREE: The more painful the story the better. It's like *Australian Idol*.
ONE: It's a selfish masochist intent to want to hear our story for the sake of hearing it .
TWO: Portrayals between the victim and survivor.

ONE: We should tweet that.
THREE: What do I do about this email regarding volunteers?
ONE: We are currently not taking volunteers.
THREE: Why not?
TWO: We are overstretched but we also don't have the capacity to ethically train, maintain volunteers. That takes time.
THREE: So we will continue to overwork ourselves because we don't have sufficient volunteers? But taking on sufficient volunteers would also overwork us?
TWO: Yep.
ONE: Put it on the agenda for the next meeting.
THREE: Okay.
THREE: When is the next meeting?
ONE: Put it on the agenda. Tick tick. Save. Next section.
THREE: [*writing an email*] 'Thank you for your inquiry.'

All back to typing at computer, silently.

TWO: Another email for refugee art projects. Everyone wants to do a refugee project now.
ONE: Now everyone wants a brown friend, now what's in vogue is a refugee friend to take around to parties. A refugee project! Wow.
THREE: 'Some of my best friends are … '
ONE: Congratulations, you organised one refugee-themed event and have x number of refugee friends, now you can never be called a racist, ignorant person again.
TWO: Funny how these projects are always *for* and not *with*.
THREE: I don't think people get that minor detail.
ONE: Artists are the worst.
THREE: Even worse than the socialists?
ONE: That's a hard one. Yes. At least the socialists know they are being political. Artists think that by waving a paintbrush or pen it'll be fine because in the end there is a nice beautiful artistic outcome. Regardless of critiques of process.
TWO: The pen is mightier than the sword but only if you know how to use it.
ONE: The pen can lead to the sword—as our refugee laws demonstrate.
TWO: The pen is a more deceptive liar, as it can write itself out of anything. Use the right words, terminology and syntax and you

can defend any bloody thing. 'We will judge who gets here and the manner in which they come.'

ONE: They always think that they are doing the discourse a favour with their 'new refugee project'.

TWO: Sometimes we don't want their help. They don't get that. They even get mad at that. Indignant almost.

THREE: Self-determination: autonomy, self-reliance, home rule, self-rule, *sovereignty*, self-sufficient.

ONE: We should tweet that!

All back to typing at computers. Silently.

THE END

A PUPPET SHOW
FOR ALL AGES

Georgia Symons

Ildiko Susany in Apocalypse Theatre Company's A PUPPET SHOW FOR ALL AGES, 2015 (Photo: Robert Catto)

A Puppet Show for All Ages was first produced by Apocalypse Theatre Company as part of the *ASYLUM* Festival at Old 505 Theatre, in February 2015, with the following creative team:

    PERFORMER   Ildiko Susany

Director, Dino Dimitriadis

Artist's Statement

I do not have lived experience of seeking asylum. When writing this piece in 2015, I did not consult with anyone with lived experience of seeking asylum. I would not write this piece today in the way I wrote it then. I likely would not write it at all. The piece was commissioned as part of Apocalypse Theatre's *Asylum* series, responding to Operation Sovereign Borders. At the time, I wanted to lend my voice to a chorus of artists speaking out against this malicious, disastrous policy. Now I understand that there are ways I can boost the voices of people directly impacted, without trying to take ownership of other people's stories, and put my name on them. As this collection concerns itself with how the Australian theatre's staging of asylum seeker stories has changed over time, I am happy and humbled that this piece has been selected for inclusion. Revisiting the piece has also been a fruitful opportunity for me to reflect on the development of my own ideas about which stories I tell, and how, and why. This is an ongoing process of reflection, and I still have a lot to learn. I hope that, in future, the Australian theatre listens to people with lived experience of seeking asylum, and prioritises their voices.

NOTE

This is a piece for one actor. It involves one character, ZEINAH, inhabiting the body of the other, ACTOR. In the moments where the ACTOR regains consciousness and talks, her lines are aligned to the right of the page.

For the purposes of this production, key stage directions are in ***bold italics***.

SCENE 1

A bare stage. Silence.

Some time passes. Then, out of the wings, **a WOMAN rushes on, screaming**. *She runs awkwardly, like she's not used to it. After the initial noise, we realise that she is screaming in delight. She pauses. She breathes. She looks down at her body. She screams with delight some more.*

A pause.

She turns to see the audience. More screams of delight.

ACTOR: AAAAAAAAAHHH!! Are you kidding? AAAAAHAHAHAHA! This is great. Oh. Oh wow, this is—This is—
This is—

She catches her breath for a second. ***She looks at her body.***

Actor—have a play here. This woman has taken possession of your body. Imagine her as very different to you physically, and then put her in your body. Ad-lib comments on what she experiences as she explores some of the following:

Is she lighter or heavier than you? Compared to her normal weight, does she feel like she's floating in your body, or does she feel weighed down?

What is your voice like compared to hers?

What is it like for her to walk in your body? Are her legs longer or shorter? What does walking feel like to her?

Are you more or less flexible than her? Can your body do party tricks that hers can't? If there's any party trick at all you can do, no matter how small, do it now. Cartwheels, double-jointed stuff, whatever you've got.

How does she feel about your clothes? How do they affect the way she moves in your body?

Gosh this is just so great, how did this—I don't know where I am. But it's good. It's really good, it's like—This is like having a puppet. This is my puppet. I can talk to you now. Incredible.

You know my parents were puppeteers. We had a little theatre in our yard and we—I can really just say whatever I want right now, can't I? This is great. The puppet theatre, I want to tell you all about it.

Mum and Dad built this tiny little puppet theatre and put it in a tent out the back of our house. I remember sneaking out to listen through the skin of the tent—it was warm, this big, thick-skinned breathing thing—and I would fall asleep next to it, the laughter and music from inside its belly rippling through my dreams. And then I'd wake up to my aunty telling me off once the show had ended, about to get stampeded by people coming out of the tent. I would run back inside, covered in all the dust that settled on me off the breeze, glowing against the darkness of my skin. I thought the dust was from somewhere else. I thought that wherever I went in my dreams, dust must be like snow there. I decided dream-snow was better than snow-snow, because it doesn't melt, or get icy, or make you cold at all, and it stays all-year round.

The little tent theatre was always packed. The tickets were cheap, and Dad let in half the town for free anyway. Most people loved the puppets and everyone hated the weather, so they came together there, and watched the ridiculous stories Mum and Dad made up. Finally, when I was ten, my Mum let me start helping out as a hostess, welcoming everyone to the show. I was crazy about it. For hours before the show, I would run my mother's comb through my straight black hair, long after I'd got all the tangles out. I would separate out each …

The* ACTOR, *whose body* ZEINAH *is inhabiting, seems to awake for a second. Her eyes widen as she sees where she is. She goes to say something, but* ZEINAH *returns.

… would—would separate out each hair, umm, and plait it into a perfect braid, then put on my best dress—the same one every day, it reeked, I almost never washed it, I was so scared of ruining it—then take my seat behind our little ticket table. I would take people's tickets and serve their mati, and from my high stool at the door-flap of the tent, I watched the show. I loved it so much, one time I—

***The* ACTOR *awakes again and tries to get sound out*—**

                                                Aaaaaaaaaa—

I remember

   A nervous giggle.

trying not to blink for a whole performance in case I missed something. The tears ran and ran down my face. The puppets looked so fragile, but they could do anything. They could tie themselves in knots and fly all over the world. They could die over and over again and then pop right back up for more. There's nothing a puppet can't do. And now I have a puppet of my own!

   ***Do your party trick again**—do a cartwheel or something, whatever trick you're good at.*

   Coming down out of the cartwheel (or finishing whatever other trick you do), **ACTOR** *awakes, dizzy.*

                                     What is … what—

Nothing. Nothing a puppet can't do. But maybe my favourite thing of all was seeing Mum and Dad reappear out of thin air for a moment in the middle of the performance. They were there the whole time, of course, but they were so—I don't know how to say it. They *were* their puppets, except then something would happen—something would fall over, or they'd catch each other's eye, and it would be them again, just for a moment. And from that one moment, you'd realise how caught up you'd been in the illusion, and then you'd get even more caught up than before.

How can I do that? I wanna show you some things. I wanna see if I can show you a bit what I'm like. Would you like that?

   Which part of me would you like to see? My hands?

   I think you'd like to see my hands. Should I show you them?

   Umm … Maybe …

   Take out a marker, ***then scribble lines all over one of your hands****. Then show this to the audience.*

It's funny to show you in this way.

   Guess I have to make do with what I've got.

   Look here. The palms. The lines.

You know my dad was sixty-five years old when I was born? Now look at these hands. Are these the hands of someone my age?

Withdraw your hand.

Which part will be next?

It won't be my face, it's too soon for that.

Much too soon, and anyway I'm sure you've seen similar things.

Photographs in papers. There have been photographers. Not many, but some. I think you'd like to see my knees. Here are my knees.

*Take out the marker and **draw some lines across one of your knees**, then offer this for the audience to look at.*

I hope I'm not making my puppet feel too much like a stripper or anything. These are my knees, look.

I'd like you to see every part of me. I think that's important. Do you like my knees? That's a very odd question, isn't it? I guess I don't expect you to have an opinion on knees.

But here, look.

Look past the hairs, look at the skin. Someone said to me once that scars are always interesting.

There's always an interesting story behind a scar. There's no interesting stories behind mine.

There's nothing behind my scars except my kneecaps.

But maybe that's not true.

Anyway I think they're like words. Scars, they're like words. They don't actually mean anything. So you can decide.

So I'm sure you'll decide.

Withdraw your knee.

What about my back?

***Turn your back to the audience.** If you're comfortable, lift your shirt to show the skin of your back.*

Here, there are no scars on my back. I hope there's no scars on her back.

The skin won't be the same colour, won't pick up light the same way, but I hope it's smooth. I hope it's a nice back like mine.

I have a nice back.

Men I've been with have told me that I have a nice back. Some say sculpted. They touch it. They lie awake touching it. I was often woken by a man touching my back in the middle of the night. But whenever I try to look in the mirror it's all twisted around. Someday I'll have to have someone take a photo.

When your face looks the way my face looks now you need to start taking pride in something.

Withdraw your back, then put your elbow in the light.

My elbows? But actually I think I prefer my forearms

*Extend your arms to **show your forearms**. With the marker, **scribble on some veins**. Through this section, get very close to the audience. In the lead-up to 'don't touch me', get so close to people that either one of them tries to touch you, or you accidentally touch them. This moment of contact wakes up the actor for a second, and she shouts the capitalised words.*

I'm pretty strong. You see the veins very clearly. The way they stick out when they're tense, when I'm tense, or when I have to use them—

DON'T TOUCH ME.

Sharply withdraw your arm. Don't give an accusatory glance to anyone in particular.

I'm—I'm sorry, it's … I'm sorry. I don't understand, what's—
I think it's important that you know me. I think it's important that you know all about me. That you know my father's hands and my scarred knees and my smooth back and my strong arms.

I just want to show you one more thing though.

I want to show you my face.

Would that be okay, if I showed you my face?

I'm sure you've seen it before

But I think this will be different

I don't think you understand just yet. So I'm going to show you my face.

Get out a large needle, threaded with coarse thread. Start to raise it towards your lips, but with immense effort, as though the body does not want you to raise your hand to your face. Struggle with this throughout:

I've thought about this a lot. I remember thinking that I wouldn't wish it upon anyone. And especially now, this puppet, so generous in letting me in, letting me take refuge in her body. It's an awful thing. Even now I feel sick, sick to my stomach and sick to hers. But I don't know how else to—you don't understand. You've seen the pictures, there are always pictures, but you don't know how I did that to my face.

I'm sure you can guess how I did it, but you don't know. I want to show you.

                                                                           No

I think it's important.
    It's quite easy.
    No, not easy.
    Not at the time.

                                                                           No

But I think about it now
    And I think that it's a good thing.
    It's a good thing that I did this to my face,

                                                                       Stop

because now there are not many things I do not know about pain.
    All kinds of pain,
    All kinds.
    And you see, because Mum and Dad …

                                                                   No, no

Because they won't ever see this face again,
    There's no other need for it, but this.
    This is the best thing I could do with my body, with my face.
    And that is another pain I understand now, too.

                                                                           No

I understand now.
    I understand now.
    I understand no—

> no no no no stop STOP

Drop the needle. *A beat. See it on the ground. Kick it away, as far as you can. Catch your breath a little.*

No I'm sorry I'm sorry. I'm sorry. That's my pain. It isn't your pain. It isn't yours to see, it isn't yours to feel, it isn't … [*Looking at the body you're in*] isn't hers. [*To yourself*] She's coming back.

Beat. Back to audience.

She has—you have—different pain. I'm sure you do. I had pain, before all of this, no life is without pain. But this pain—my pain—this doesn't happen at home. It doesn't happen in nice places like this. I'm trying to put my pain in the wrong place. This is far-away pain. And I'm sure some of you are concerned, or just curious, I'm sure some of you would like to see more of my body. But this is just it—you don't have to. This pain doesn't have to come anywhere near your lives.

Look down at the body. Take your time.

What a beautiful thing she is. What a beautiful place to live. Pale, and light. You could really stand out in this body, or you could disappear. It would be completely up to you. I could just walk around in this body. I could just walk around. I could just walk down the street.

Take a moment to enjoy this thought.

Do the party trick—the cartwheel or the double-jointed thing or whatever. Smile.

I could talk, and people would listen. You would listen. You'd hear me out.

> Get out.

No, please, I just—
  Please, just another—just let me—please—

> Get out get out—

ZEINAH *is pushed out, and* **the ACTOR** *regains possession of her body. She collapses into a chair, or onto the floor. She breathes. She pays the audience no heed. She catches her breath. Silence.*

She looks absently around the stage. She gets up, walks around slowly. **She finds the needle. She picks it up**, *and sits down, in the chair or on the floor. She stares at it. Hand trembling, but not as much as before, she raises it to her lip.* **She presses the sharp point of the needle against her skin**—*not enough to pierce, but almost. She winces as she does this, holds it there for a long time.* **Calmly, she takes the pressure off. She lowers the needle.** *She looks at it. She puts it back in her pocket.*

Her breathing returns to normal.

THE END

WE ALL KNOW WHAT'S HAPPENING

Samara Hersch and Lara Thoms

Bridie Noonan, Eve Nixon, Lazar Feldman, Finley Owen, Tove Due and Venu Elisaia in Arts House's WE ALL KNOW WHAT'S HAPPENING, 2017 (Photo: Bryony Jackson)

Introduction

The figure of the child in refugee advocacy has a vexed history. Images such as that of toddler Alan Kurdi, who perished when fleeing Syria for Turkey, can shock the world into action, leading to international pledges and press, and a 3,000 per cent increase in charitable donations (Dumas 2016). However, focusing on women and young children often coincides with a problematic emphasis on vulnerability and victimhood rather than agency, and caters to the racist nation-state by crafting a carefully non-threatening image of refugees (see, for instance, Malkki 1996; Rajaram 2002; Szczepanikova 2009). How then can artists make ethical, effective and affective art about refugee children without falling into the same traps? *We All Know What's Happening* took on this challenge by collaborating with Australian children to devise a performance about their peers in immigration detention on the Republic of Nauru.

The performance came about when co-creators Samara Hersch and Lara Thoms saw the image of Kurdi. Hersch said, 'there was a deep kind of empathy that was coming from the media', adding, 'I found this personally very confronting ... what was happening. [And] I was interested in how children can speak about questions of justice differently to adults' (von Einem 2019). In 2016, Hersch and Thoms put out a call for young people to respond to the provocation of what they would like to see changed in the world and how they would go about producing this change (von Einem 2019). From here, seven Melbourne-based young people aged between 10 and 17 years became the cast and co-creators of *We All Know What's Happening*.

The performance fuses the conventions of a school history lesson and pantomime to trace the 100-million-year history of Nauru. The government often deliberately frames Australia's offshore detention sites as obscure, far-off places and media reports about them are often decontextualised, dehistoricised and delocalised. The regional and historical forces that have seen each instrumentalised as sites of torture financed by the Australian government are conveniently disregarded. Yet each of these places has their own distinct history, culture and peoples. *We All Know What's Happening* attends to the detailed and specific history of Nauru, from the mining of phosphate found on the island from thousands of years of hot weather and seagull faeces, through multiple invasions and world wars to the unfortunate funding of a musical flop about Leonardo Da Vinci. In doing so, it addresses the absurd circumstances that have led the Micronesian country to go from being known as Pleasant Island—and the wealthiest country per capita in the world—to a site of brutal abuse where asylum seekers are held captive indefinitely (Dauvergne 2019).

There is a tension between these bleak facts and the bright stage. Early in the work, as if to anticipate the audience reaction, one of the young actors announces that the following incidents are facts, even when they seem stranger than fiction. The brightly coloured cardboard props are endearingly homemade and the descriptions of colonial extraction and neocolonial expansion are gentle and age-appropriate, but the overall effect is unsettling. Slowly but surely, it becomes clear that the young artists have adopted the aesthetics of a school play not to address the children in the audience, but rather to school the adults about human rights and justice. Far from depoliticising the refugee issue then, they repoliticise it: examining it from the perspective of young people, with a focus on young people via a deliberately and deceptively youthful aesthetic. Indeed, they share stories of their political activities. For instance, some of the performers are members of the 'children for children' movement which sees young people doing 'detention for detention'—voluntarily sitting in silence for an hour in after-school detention to demonstrate their solidarity with children held in offshore detention. That these artist-activists are too young to vote, or even to remember a time before these policies were implemented, only adds to the stories' impact.

If one point of tension is between the child performers and their adult audiences, then another is between the performers and their counterparts in Nauru. The cast weave their personal narratives throughout the play, contrasting their memories of birthdays at fun parks and beach houses with the experiences of asylum seekers. This tension is brought to a head in the third act, when one of the actors stops the show and asks anyone in the audience under the age of 13 years to leave the theatre. These children are then escorted to an adjacent room, where they watch a child-friendly third act, in which the performers share their favourite clause from the United Nations Convention on the Rights of the Child. Meanwhile, the two performers who are under the age of 13 raise their hands and a stagehand enters to place noise-cancelling headphones on them, which they wear for the remainder of the show. From here, the older performers share some of the contents of the Nauru files, albeit in modified form. These include instances of sexual assault, self-immolation, and suicide. The contrast is confronting: Australia subjects refugee children to assault, abuse and indefinite detention, but protects other children from even *hearing about* these experiences. In other words, only some children have the right to be children. This lead one reviewer to state, 'here the performance strikes its greatest chord' (Hunt 2017). It also gave new meaning to the title: we all know what's happening, yes, but some of us know more than others. And the people who know the most are, disturbingly, refugees who are mere children.

The absence of refugee children is made palpable via the production's skilful dramaturgy. In a scene towards the end of the play, seven microphones are placed on an otherwise empty stage while an audio track plays of asylum seeker children sharing their thoughts, such as what they want to be when they grow up and what freedom means to them. The cast then brings more and more microphones onto the stage, one at a time. Slowly, the stage starts to fill with microphones standing in for those not able to be there, reminding us of how Australia's policy has individually and collectively affected children in these detention centres.

As a play about children, co-developed and performed by children, *We All Know What's Happening* is a unique addition to the refugee theatre landscape. Reviewers praised the show as a 'remarkable insight into Nauru through children's eyes' (Woodhead 2017), a 'work that is resona[nt], powerful and of the times' (Hunt 2017) and 'an outstanding artistic format for political urgency' (Zürcher Theater Spektakel 2019). The play won Best Production and Contemporary and Experimental Performance at the 2018 Green Room Awards. In 2019, the piece also won the Patronage and Audience prizes at the Zürcher Theater Spektakel (see Zürcher Theater Spektakel 2019) and was invited to be presented at Theater Der Welt (Theatre of the World) in Germany in

2020. Such international exposure and acclaim are relatively rare for Australian refugee-related theatre.

We All Know What's Happening never mentions political parties, and only refers to politicians by their first names, subverting their power and ensuring that we focus on the people detained on Nauru. In doing so, the performance confronts power, holds space and challenges the contradictions in how we see ourselves.

Tania Cañas and Caroline Wake

References

Dauvergne, Peter. 2019. 'A Dark History of the World's Smallest Island Nation'. *The MIT Press Reader*, 22 July. https://thereader.mitpress.mit.edu/dark-history-nauru/.

Dumas, Daisy. 2016. 'Alan Kurdi Photo Triggered 3000 per cent Rise in Australian Charity to World Vision: Tim Costello'. *Sydney Morning Herald*, 4 February. https://www.smh.com.au/national/alan-kurdi-photo-triggered-wave-of-australian-charity-to-world-vision-tim-costello-20160203-gmkgky.html.

Hersch, Samara and Lara Thoms. 2017. 'Artist Statement'. In *We All Know What's Happening by Samara Hersch and Lara Thoms Show Program*. 2017. Arts House, July. http://www.artshouse.com.au/wp-content/uploads/2017/07/We-All-Know-Whats-Happening-by-Samara-Hersch-and-Lara-Thoms-Show-Program.pdf.

Hunt, Michael. 2017. 'We All Know What's Happening'. *Toorak Times*, 21 July. https://tagg.com.au/know-whats-happening/.

Malkki, Liisa H. 1996. 'Speechless Emissaries: Refugees, Humanitarianism, and Dehistoricization'. *Cultural Anthropology* 11, no. 3: 377–404. http://www.jstor.org/stable/656300.

Rajaram, Prem Kumar. 2002. 'Humanitarianism and Representation of the Refugee'. *Journal of Refugee Studies* 15, no. 3: 247–64. https://doi.org/10.1093/jrs/15.3.247.

Szczepanikova, Alice. 2009. 'Beyond Helping': Gender and Relations of Power in Non-Governmental Assistance to Refugees'. *Journal of International Women's Studies* 11, no. 3: 19–33.

von Einem, Johnny. 2019. 'Refugees, Australia, and Nauru, as Told by Schoolchildren'. *CityMag*, 7 February. https://citymag.indaily.com.au/culture/we-all-know-whats-happening-vitalstatistix-samara-hersch-lara-thoms/.

Woodhead, Cameron. 2017. 'We All Know What's Happening: A Remarkable Insight into Nauru through the Eyes of Children'. *The Age*, 20 July. https://www.theage.com.au/entertainment/we-all-know-whats-happening-a-remarkable-insight-into-nauru-through-the-eyes-of-children-20170720-gxf60e.html.

Zürcher Theater Spektakel. 2019. 'ZKB Patronage Prize: Statement of the Jury'. Theater Spektakel. https://www.theaterspektakel.ch/en/about-us/zkb-prizes/statements-of-the-jury-2018/.

We All Know What's Happening was first produced at Arts House Melbourne, on 19 July 2017, with the following creative team:

Co-Creators: Samara Hersch and Lara Thoms
Performers and Creators: Bridie Noonan, Eve Nixon, Allegra Di Lallo, Lazar Feldman, Finley Owen, Tove Due, and Venu Elisaia
Designer: Romanie Harper with Lara Thoms
Lighting Design: Jen Hector
Music Direction/Sound Design: Marco Cher-Gibard
Pianist/Sound Collaborator: Grace Ferguson
Production Coordinator and Youth Support: Prue Clark
Stage Manager: Olivia Bishop
Consultation: Save the Children and Arnold Zable

Supported by City of Melbourne, Creative Victoria and Australia Council for the Arts.

Subsequent seasons: Campbelltown Arts Centre, Sydney (2018), Vitalstatistix, Adelaide (2019), Zürcher Theater Spektakel (2019), Nooderzon Festival (2019)

For these seasons, the creative team included Cassandra Fumi (Stage Manager/ Show Director and Youth Support) and Tennessee Mynott-Rudland (Stage Manager) with the following performers:

Allegra Di Lallo, Lazar Feldman, Finley Owen, Tove Due, Venu Elisaia, Theo Boltman, and Casper Plum

This script reflects this most recent cast.

Artists' Statement

We All Know What's Happening is a response to Australia's ongoing colonial relationship with Nauru. From very early phosphate mining to negotiations around refugee detention centres, our country has literally placed itself in the middle of this tiny pacific island, adding to a long list of complex, cruel and absurd injustices.

Australian school children have only recently begun to learn about Australia's own history of invasion and exploitation towards our First Nations People. This work hopes to extend the awareness of our country's questionable behaviour across the Pacific and our violation of basic human rights toward asylum seekers.

This work premiered in 2017, more than four years after the Australian government announced that 'Asylum seekers who come here by boat without a visa will never be settled in Australia'. This effort to keep people out of sight and therefore out of mind is what our work hopes to challenge. We, like many others, want to keep this conversation on the table and end this unnecessary cycle of trauma that is happening in our name.

Although we often feel the need to protect Australian children from atrocities performed by our country, there is a particular tension when these atrocities involve other children of the same age. Throughout this process we worked with several incredible young people who are thoughtful, political and deeply concerned. As we toured the work nationally and internationally, these young people spoke passionately to local audiences outside of the performances, raising awareness and solidarity across geographical borders.

Whilst *We All Know What's Happening* plays with traditional and sometimes satirical forms such as the musical and school history lesson, the politics of this work are intentionally palpable. What we didn't expect was that the despair we felt at the beginning of our process shift to inspiration as we witness young people dedicated to changing Australia's policies and seeing children their age find justice.

ROLES

We All Know What's Happening is performed by seven children aged 10–17, who may not have performance experience. Diversity of backgrounds and genders is preferred, as is an interest in activism and human rights.

NARRATOR 1, aged 10–12, confident and earnest delivery

NARRATOR 2, aged 10–12, confident and earnest delivery

NARRATOR 3, aged 15–17, confident, calm and politically aware delivery

CHILD 1, 14–17, confident storyteller and singer

CHILD 2, any age 10–17

CHILD 3, any age 10–17

CHILD 4 / LEONARDO, any age 10–17, confident and animated in movement

STYLE

We All Know What's Happening should appear to be in the style of a traditional school play starring 10- to 17-year-olds. Previous iterations have been accompanied by live piano played by an adult pianist, who in Act One and Act Two performs a mash up of colonial songs, national anthems and pop songs such as ABBA's 'Money Money Money' to further highlight the naive and gradually cynical tone of the work. In Act Three (after the show stop), the pianist leaves the piano and joins the audience. The performers play themselves and avoid an overtly theatrical delivery of text. The style is intentionally earnest and simplistic in its initial appearance, yet the underlying irony and political message begins to reveal itself in the following acts.

DESIGN AND SETTING

The set and costume for *We All Know What's Happening* should appear to be in the style of a traditional school play. The main costumes are school uniforms, with the renaissance costumes happily incongruous. The set pieces are simple and most props are made out of painted cardboard. The floor is lined with yellow and blue carpet tiles to suggest an island. These tiles are consistently removed throughout the show to suggest mining of the land.

STRUCTURE

PROLOGUE: An excerpt from *Leonardo the Musical: A Portrait of Love* (1993), performed in full renaissance outfits and lip-synced.

ACT ONE: Naive school musical. From 1 million years ago to 1951, with the signing of the UN Convention relating to the status of Refugees

ACT TWO: From 1968, the year of Nauru's Independence, to the early 2000s. Please note that this act is interrupted by a show stop by CHILD 4. They ask that children under 13 years old in the audience leave the theatre, together with cast member CHILD 1 and the pianist. These children will move out of the theatre for a more 'child friendly' experience. This is usually situated in a room close by to the theatre, made comfortable for child audiences, with a tent like structure made of bed sheets and pillows and a screen to share a video made by the cast—which shares their favourite Rights of the Child. Here CHILD 3 reads out a picture book made by the cast, that shares the same facts that the audience is watching in Act Three, but with more child friendly language, and omitting more graphic facts. The children also discuss the United Nations Convention on the Rights of the Child.

ACT THREE: From early 2000s to current day. During this act the lived experience of the performers begins to interweave with the historical facts. At the end of this act, the child audience under 13 return to the theatre.

ACT FOUR: Installation of microphones and the audio of voices from children who were refugees in Nauru, recorded in 2015-2017.

PROLOGUE

The stage is clear. Slowly seven choreographed dancing/singing CHILDREN *in basic Renaissance costumes arrive and lip-sync to the song 'Renaissance' from* Leonardo the Musical: A Portrait of Love *(1993).*

The performers very slowly exit the stage, looking directly at the audience with a deadpan expression.

Curtains close.

ACT ONE

NARRATOR 1: Hi everyone. Today we are doing a lesson about a small island called Nauru. You may not think that everything we are about to tell you is true, but believe me, all of this is one hundred per cent facts. So let's get started.

One million years ago there is an Island. This Island is a small tropical paradise with palm trees, coconuts, crystal blue water and bright sunshine.

There are no people on this Island, but it is visited by birds who use it as a toilet stop when taking long journeys across the ocean.

NARRATOR 1 *plays the bird whistle.*

A CHILD *dressed as a seagull walks across the stage. In the background, two children make water with fabric. The child in the seagull costume stops in the centre and drops a small ball of white paper behind them (to indicate bird poo).*

Sometime later the first signs of humans appear on the Island.

The humans speak lots of different versions of a language called 'Dorerin Naoero'.

The humans living on the Island divide themselves into twelve clans. Most of these clans believe in a female Goddess called Eijebong.

NARRATOR 1 *strikes chimes. A* CHILD *brings a cardboard star onstage.*

The people invent a special way to farm fish. They take the fish out of the ocean and put them into a lagoon, which makes them easy to catch.

A CHILD *brings a cardboard fish that swims across the stage.*

These humans get their food and all that they need from the Island.

Beat.

Hundreds of years later, a British whale hunter arrives. He has a look around and calls this place 'Pleasant Island'.

A CHILD *enters as an invader with a British flag hat and places a sign on stage saying 'Pleasant Island'.*

Other whalers arrive and stop over at the Island to drink some water and eat some fish.

They start trading with the people on the Island. In exchange for food, they give them alcohol and guns.

These things disrupt the peace of the clans living on the Island.

Beat.

Shortly after, Germany arrives and invades the Island.

A CHILD *enters with German flag hat on and places flag on sign saying 'Pleasant Island'.*

They change the Island's name to Nawodo and they ban traditional dancing as they believe it is too pagan.

The birds keep visiting and keep going to the toilet.

Bird whistle again from NARRATOR 1.

A CHILD *dressed as a seagull walks across the stage and deposits a paper poo. Behind the bird,* CHILDREN *make water with fabric.*

During this time, an Australian man called Henry pops over to the Island and notices some strange looking wood.

A CHILD *crosses the stage with a microscope.*

He plans on making children's marbles from this wood but he's too lazy so instead he uses it as a doorstop in his office.

A few years after that, a man called Albert takes another look at Henry's strange wooden doorstop and decides it is so strange that he needs to do some tests on it.

He puts it under the microscope and discovers the wood is actually phosphate.

The CHILD *with the telescope lifts one of the carpet tiles to reveal a glowing light.*

This discovery leads to an even bigger discovery.

It turns out that because of all the birds pooing over all the millions of years, together with the warm sun and air, phosphate is everywhere on the Island!

> CHILDREN *discover phosphate (by revealing more glowing lights under the carpet tiles).*

Germany begins mining.

> TWO CHILDREN *with German flag hats start 'mining'—removing carpet squares from the ground.*
>
> THREE CHILDREN *enter with AUS, NZ, UK hats and place flags on sign saying 'Pleasant Island'.*

Soon after, the rest of the world enters into a big war.
The Island is captured by Australia, New Zealand and the UK.
These countries take over the mining. They sell the phosphate to the rest of the world and keep the money.

> *Beat.*

You're probably thinking—What is phosphate? And why does everyone want it?

> THREE CHILDREN *display cardboard bones, teeth and fertiliser.*

Phosphorus is important to all living things. It helps create DNA, blood cells, teeth and bones.
It is important for growing food since it is one of three nutrients used in fertiliser.

> *Beat.*

Then the world enters into a second big war.

> *A* CHILD *enters with Japanese flag, places the flag on the sign saying 'Pleasant Island'.*

This time Japan captures the Island.
These invaders force the people of the Island to work for very long hours and feed them hardly any food.

> *A cardboard boat floats across the stage.*

During this time Islanders who were suffering from leprosy are loaded onto boats by the Japanese and are towed out to sea and when no-one is looking, they are sunk.

> *The boat disappears under the water fabric.*

Despite this, the people of the Island successfully grow aubergine, corn, pumpkin, and sweet potato.

> THREE CHILDREN *display cardboard aubergine, corn, pumpkin, and sweet potato.*

The birds keep on visiting and keep on pooing.

> NARRATOR 1 *plays the bird whistle.*
>
> *A* CHILD *dressed as a seagull walks across the stage and deposits a paper poo. Behind the seagull children make water with fabric.*

Then Australia and its friends invade the Island again.

They continue to mine whatever is left of the phosphate.

> *UK, NZ, AUS flags mine the carpet squares.*

All of this mining makes the Island very difficult to live on.

Most of the land is covered in a rocky moonscape.

So, Australia offers to relocate the entire population to a new Island off the Great Barrier Reef.

People living there call the Islanders bad names and say they don't want them.

> *A* CHILD *holding a cardboard fish crosses the stage, alongside a speech bubble that says 'Rack off'.*

But the people on the Island decide they don't want to be moved, as this Island is their home, and they would prefer to look after it.

> NARRATOR 1 *plays chimes.*
>
> *Beat.*

A few years later, a group of countries get together in Switzerland to talk about the second big war that just happened.

They decide to make an agreement about what to do when innocent people no longer feel safe in their country.

The agreement says that people who are forced to leave their country to find a new home will not get in trouble.

Australia, The Netherlands, Switzerland, America and most other countries take out a pen and sign this agreement.

> CHILDREN *wearing flags of UN countries shake hands. The* NARRATORS *swap by going over to the lectern, shaking hands and pretending to sign something with a giant paper pen.*

ACT TWO

NARRATOR 2: Then, around ten years later, a big event happens.
 The Island becomes an independent nation.
 They finally get to take control of their Island again.
 There is a celebration!
 The Island gets a flag and a national anthem, and there are barbecues and picnics.

> *A* CHILD *places a Nauruan flag on the sign.*

Not long after, tourists from all around the world start to visit the Island for their summer holidays.

> *The song 'Concrete and Clay,' by the band Unit 4 + 2, is played. (Tommy Moeller, the lead singer of Unit 4 + 2, developed the musical about the life of Leonardo da Vinci.)*

The Island starts to smell like perfume and cigarettes.

> *Children become tourists, driving cardboard cars and playing golf with a cardboard golf stick. Some have a cardboard camera and cardboard cocktail glass and cigarette.*

The Island puts the mining money into a Trust, pretty much making every one of its inhabitants an individual millionaire.
 Everyone on the Island gets health care and education.
 A lot of people buy a car, even though the drive around the entire island doesn't last much more than thirty minutes.
 The leader of the Island buys a Lamborghini but then because of his size—he can't fit into it.
 The Lamborghini rots and rusts in the sun.
 Lots of people get air conditioners and a satellite TV and watch shows from far away like 'Skippy the Bush Kangaroo'.

> *A* CHILD *with a cardboard kangaroo tail and ears hops across the stage.*

A golf course is built with nine holes, taking up a lot of the land on the Island that has not been mined.
 People on holiday bring their golf clubs and practise their swings.

Now there are traffic jams on the tiny Island.

Then, a man living in Australia, called Duke, who is a songwriter but works in a bank, puts up his hand.

Beat. Music stops and performers freeze.

He offers to give the Island some financial advice.

He thinks this money could be invested to make more money!

PERFORMERS *run off stage and return with paper planes.*

Duke convinces the Island to buy not one, not two, but a dozen giant planes, which seems unnecessary since the Island has a population of only eight thousand people.

CHILDREN *holding paper planes cross the stage.*

He also recommends that the Island spend nineteen million dollars to build an impressive fifty-two-storey building in Melbourne.

This is one of the tallest buildings at the time.

A CHILD *enters dressed as a cardboard skyscraper.*

He then recommends the Island invests one-point-two million to save Melbourne's football team, The Lions, from having to become The Kangaroos.

CHILDREN *with a cardboard football run around the stage.*

Then our friend Duke has a new idea!

There is a dramatic stop in action and music.

He suggests an investment into a new large-scale musical!

A musical that will tour London's West End with colourful costumes and big sets!

CHILDREN *frantically change into renaissance costumes on stage.*

Duke himself starts to write the musical about Leonardo Da Vinci falling in love with the Mona Lisa!

This play is four hours long and in Act Three the Mona Lisa gets pregnant and Leonardo Da Vinci gets murdered.

Musical repeat: CHILDREN *lip-sync in a more sinister, gothic style. With one of the performers appearing pregnant.*

A CHILD *enacts stabbing Leonardo, who collapses on the floor. Eventually he gets up and exits, defeated.*

Then the people who live on the Island hear that they are spending the equivalent of seven million dollars on this production.

They form a protest at the airport.

Their leaders board a plane to fly to London for the opening night.

The people of the Island grab onto the wings of the aeroplane.

They have had enough of this kind of spending.

CHILDREN *hold protest signs reading 'Boo,' 'Zero Stars' etc.*

The musical doesn't do very well, with some reviews suggesting it was one of the biggest disasters in the history of London theatre.

The Island loses all of its investment money spent on the musical.

Beat.

Now the leaders of the Island begin to worry.

This time some people from Russia come up with an idea.

They suggest the Island opens a bank.

A desk is pushed onstage with a desk fan. A CHILD *starts to slowly throw paper money into the fan, so that it makes a big mess on the floor.*

A married couple from America called Lucy and Peter put up their hands to help run this bank from New York.

TWO CHILDREN *wearing hats with American flags, holding hands, cross the stage and wave to the audience.*

Some Russian businessmen find out about this idea.

They decide to put not seventy million, but seventy billion dollars into this bank.

Another four hundred and fifty banks open on the Island.

All of the banks are located in one small shack with a fan and a single computer.

Then the leaders of the Island start to sell passports for lots of money to people in other countries.

The people buying the passports have never even been to the Island.

Then the Island's president gets sick and is flown to the USA for a heart operation.

While he is in hospital important people visit him and tell him he had better shut down the banks and the passports.

He says yes as he wheeled into surgery, nodding his head.

CHILD *dressed as a doctor, enters and pulls the plug on the fan.*

That same year the USA and its friends, including Australia and Europe, get involved in another big war on the other side of the world.

TWO CHILDREN *cross the stage with cardboard machine guns. They smile at the audience as they cross the stage. Sound of two loud gunshots is played.*

Because of this war, thousands of people are forced to flee their homes.

Tove starts kindergarten and likes watching *Dr Who*. [*Text can be replaced with the child performer's personal history from around 2008.*]

On seas far away, a friendly Norwegian man saves four hundred people whose small boat was sinking on their way to Australia, by inviting them onto his big ship.

An Australian politician named John decides he does not want these people in Australia and forces them to stay on the hot ship in the middle of the ocean for many days.

The Norwegian man shares his small amount of food and water with the hundreds of people on his ship.

He keeps calling Australia for help, but no-one answers his call.

The boat crosses the stage with a captain on a cardboard mobile phone.

Soon after, at a barbeque in Australia, an immigration minister called Amanda has an idea!

Instead of helping the people on the boats she decides to write a song!

She calls it 'Under Southern Stars', and denies it is meant to replace the national anthem.

CHILD 1 *takes centre stage and earnestly sings the lyrics to 'Under Southern Stars' by Amanda Vanstone.*

A CHILD *interrupts boldly. Music and lighting shifts to feel like a 'show stop'.*

CHILD 3: Stop! Can we please stop! Theo (performer)—that's enough. That's enough, thank you! Grace (pianist)—can you stop please.

Grace, I said stop please.

Can I have the house lights up?

Thank you, we've had enough.

So we have come to a point in the show where some of the content has been deemed inappropriate for people thirteen years of age and under.

So can I get everyone in the room thirteen and under to please put up their hand?

NARRATOR 1 *and* NARRATOR 2 *put up their hands.*

Thank you. Could you all please stand up?

Okay so you all will be coming with my friend to a different room, where you will have a more age-appropriate experience.

So please come and meet over here.

Again I really need to stress that no-one thirteen and under can be left here in the room.

Okay ready? Let's go.

We observe younger children from the audience leave their seats and families and exit the theatre in silence.

House lights down.

ACT THREE

The stage is now filled with discarded props and costumes. At least half the carpet tiles have been removed.

NARRATOR 3: Back on the Island, fresh water starts to run out.

Eighty per cent of the Island is now a series of mines leaving only twenty per cent of the Island to live on.

Electricity exists for only four hours a day from a generator.

That makes for twenty very hot hours a day.

It even stops raining on the Island.

Clouds in the backdrop disappear.

Australia starts discovering hundreds of people from faraway places on small boats in their waters.

While this has happened before, Australia decides that this time it doesn't want these people and comes up with another idea.

Australia pays the Island millions of dollars to build a centre with high fences right in the middle of the Island.

Australia makes the people, including the children, who had travelled on the boats, live there with no idea when they will get out.

Australia sends security guards to the Island to watch over the people who are locked up there.

NARRATOR 1 *and* NARRATOR 2 *(who have noise-cancelling headphones on) enter the stage, guided by the older performer who was wearing the kangaroo tail. They stand in the centre, as security guards.*

Despite the agreement in Switzerland the security guards tell the people they are all illegal.

One of the security guards is called Michael and his only previous experience is managing a McDonald's.

CHILD 4 *enters and sits down.*

Then Lazar is born at eleven forty-five in the morning. During the labour, his parents were watching a reality TV show called *Big Brother* and wondering who would get voted out. [*Text may be replaced with the child performer's personal history from around 2004.*]

The Island completely gets rid of fruit flies which is a first for the Pacific region.

CHILD 2 *enters and sits down.*

Casper is born at home in a birth pool. [*Text may be replaced with the child performer's personal history from around 2006.*]

Finley is born a few weeks early, surprising their parents. [*Text may be replaced with the child performer's personal history from around 2006.*]

Then, some teachers go over and set up a school for those locked up on the Island.

But a book with a picture of a kangaroo in it gets confiscated for encouraging hope.

Kangaroo hops around the stage briefly.

Then it is discovered that the people on the Island are some of the sickest in the world, from the food and alcohol introduced by the whalers all those years ago.

Then a girl my age, who is forced to live on the Island, tells one of the security guards that she cannot sleep because there is a rat in her tent.

Soon after the Miss Independence Beauty Pageant is held on the Island with contestants including Miss Transfield, Miss Alpha Security and Miss Western Union.

Both traditional clothing and evening gowns are worn.

Back on the Island, a restaurant called Bondi Beach opens serving hot chips.

That year Allegra is born. [*Text may be replaced with the child performer's personal history from around 2006.*]

Then a man locked up on the Island who has lost all hope sets himself on fire.

This same year Lazar gets his appendix out and Venu is born. [*Text may be replaced with the child performer's personal history from around 2006.*]

Allegra starts kindergarten and the following year she learns how to ride a bicycle. [*Text may be replaced with the child performer's personal history from around 2007.*]

Ten female weightlifters from the Island win Commonwealth Games medals including three bronze, five silver and two gold.

Then a child locked up on the Island tells someone that a security guard has grabbed his private parts just outside his tent.

An Australian politician called Peter visits the school on the Island.

He says nice things about the school but then decides to close it down the following week.

A new cafeteria, only for the security guards, replaces the school.

A CHILD *security guard eats a donut.*

Around this time, Finley goes on holiday with their family to Kangaroo Island and sees a giant lizard. [*Text may be replaced with the child performer's personal history from around 2014.*]

The performer dressed as the kangaroo jumps around unenthusiastically, then sits down.

Soon after, a young woman who is locked up on the Island ties a rope to the beam above her tent.

The birds keep visiting the Island and keep going to the toilet.

NARRATOR 1 *plays the bird whistle.*

A politician named Malcolm speaks to a doctor who is working on the Island.

He tells him that if he talks about what he sees, he will go to jail for two years.

Then a group of young people locked up on the Island sew their lips together.

Back in Australia, people discover that to keep a single person on Pleasant Island costs them half a million dollars each year.

CHILD 2 *and* 4 *begin to slowly start tidying the space and moving props offstage.*

Then Venu has his birthday at a theme park by the beach.

VENU *and* ALLEGRA *(the two performers under twelve) are instructed to remove their noise-cancelling headphones by one of the older performers. Venu is given a microphone. While he speaks, some of the other performers start clearing the props from the stage.*

NARRATOR 1: Okay so for my seventh birthday I went to Luna Park with my family and the first ride we went on was the Carnival of Horrors. So um, we went in and there was this glass cage around us. So then a couple of seconds later there was this guy in a gorilla costume, and he popped out of nowhere and scared me and my sister and my cousins. So they ended up bailing out on me at the next emergency exit. I wanted to leave as well but my mum said I couldn't because I had to have a 'special' birthday experience. So I ended up crying and my brother had to carry me out the rest of the way. [*Text may be replaced with the child performer's personal story about their experience of fear, can be semi improvised.*]

NARRATOR 2: I was on holidays with my family, down at my beach house. My brother had set up this cage to catch this cheeky wild rabbit that was eating all of our vegetables and digging holes everywhere. But when we woke up in the morning, instead of a rabbit being in the cage there was a snoring koala. So we decided to wake him up and set him free in some nearby gum trees, and we never saw him again. [*Text may be replaced with the child performer's personal story about their experience of fear, can be semi improvised.*]

NARRATOR 3: Around that time, Casper gets put in detention for stealing ice cream from the school canteen. [*Text may be replaced with the child performer's recent history, around ideas of school detention.*]

NARRATOR 3: Then a newspaper prints hundreds of files about Pleasant Island.

These files are thousands of pages long and detail abuse and violence against the people trapped on the Island.

Stories involving children our age make up more than half of the reports.

Then some Australian children create a group called Children for Children to raise awareness for children's rights around the world.

Their first action invites school students who haven't done anything wrong to crash their own after-school detention in solidarity with refugee children in detention.

Then a group of Australian school kids voluntarily sit in silence for one hour in their different school detentions.

Back on the Island, the birds keep visiting and keep going to the toilet.

NARRATOR 1 *plays the bird whistle.*

Then Australia pays six million dollars to some filmmakers to make a feature film to deter people from travelling by boat to Australia.

The film is in Arabic with English subtitles.

Then there is a sickness on the Island.

A lot of the kids can't get out of bed, eat, clean themselves or speak. Doctors call this Traumatic Withdrawal Syndrome.

CHILD 2 *or one of the performers receives the microphone.*

CHILD 2: Then some Australian kids attend a children's protest. Some speak at the rally to hundreds of people. I carry a sign that says, 'No humans are illegal'.

NARRATOR 3: Not long after, all of the doctors are suddenly told they must leave the Island immediately.

The politicians begin to feel pressured and decide to let some of the kids finally come to Australia for treatment.

These kids are scattered around the country in different kinds of detention with no certainty of where they will end up next.

Most of them cannot afford the psychological care they need.

Then a recent president of the Island is also sent to Australia to see a doctor.

On his deathbed he thinks about Pleasant Island and tells everyone that he regrets signing a deal with the devil.

A girl recently had her twelfth birthday inside an Australian detention centre.

A security guard stopped a cake from being brought in.

Beat.

Back on Pleasant Island some deep-sea miners arrive from Canada and go for a swim

The birds keep visiting and keep going to the toilet.

NARRATOR 1 *plays the bird whistle.*

The CHILDREN *all begin to help slowly empty the space of props and carpet squares.*

CHILD 2 *speaks into the microphone that is on the floor—*

CHILD 2: Hi my name is Casper and I'm interested in photography. [*Text may be replaced with the current child performer's name and interests.*]

I'm speaking for a fourteen-year-old boy, my age. Boat number censored.

He likes Minecraft and listening to Eminem.

After speaking these lines CHILD 2 *exits the stage and immediately returns with a microphone on a stand. They place it in the spot where they were speaking.*

CHILD 3: My name is Finley; I am into going to the beach and playing guitar. [*Text may be replaced with the current child performer's name and interests.*]

I am speaking on behalf of a fourteen-year-old boy my age. Boat number censored.

His favourite singer is Justin Bieber. His favourite game is football and when he grows up, he wants to be an expert football player.

After speaking these lines CHILD 1 *exits the stage and immediately returns with a microphone stand. They place it in the spot where they were speaking.*

NARRATOR 2 *takes the microphone.*

NARRATOR 2: My name is Allegra.

I have two chocolate and coffee coloured Burmese cats named Mimi and Lorna. I am speaking on behalf of a twelve-year-old girl my age because it is illegal for her to be here. [*Text may be replaced with the child performer's name and interests.*]

Boat number censored. Her favourite song is 'I'm Yours' by Jason Mraz. When she is older, she wants to be a policeman so that she can have power.

NARRATOR 2 exits the stage and immediately returns with a microphone on a stand. They place it in the spot where they were speaking.

By this stage the performance space should gradually be cleared of all the carpet tiles and props—leaving an empty stage. The remaining PERFORMERS *bring on the remaining microphones on stands and carefully place them on the stage. There should be seven microphone stands. The* CHILDREN *then exit the stage.*

ACT FOUR

One CHILD *remains onstage and speaks to the audience from the main microphone.*

CHILD 3: Then we tried to make contact with seven young people our age who were once forced to live on the Island. We asked them questions about what they thought was fair and unfair and about themselves, about freedom, power and other things.

Now some of those kids are in Australian detention, others, we don't know where they are, and some have turned eighteen and are still stuck on the Island.

>CHILD 3 *exits. Lighting change to focus on seven microphones. Then voice recordings from interviews with children stuck on Nauru are played.*

MIC 1: [*voiceover*] 'Hello I am a seventeen-years-old boy.'

MIC 2: [*voiceover*] 'I am a ten-years-old girl.'

MIC 3: [*voiceover*] 'Hello I am eleven-years-old girl.'

MIC 4: [*voiceover*] 'I'm a boy, I'm ten years old.'

MIC 5: [*voiceover*] 'Hello I am eleven-years-old boy.'

MIC 6: [*voiceover*] 'Hello I'm a boy, fifteen years old.'

MIC 7: [*voiceover*] 'I'm fifteen-years-old girl.'

>CHILDREN *continue to bring microphones on stands onto the stage one by one. They first bring out around five. Then once the performers are off stage again we hear:*

MIC 1: [*voiceover*] 'To do what you want and what you want to be—it's fair but when you want to be something, and you can't it's unfair.'

>*A second round of microphones are placed on the stage by the* CHILDREN. *Once the stage is empty of performers again voice recordings continue.*

MIC 2: [*voiceover*] 'Freedom is good to have but as long as it doesn't … it benefits everyone—not just you—you don't do something with your freedom that hurts the others. The benefit has to be for everyone—not only for you.'

A third round of microphones are placed on the stage by the CHILDREN. *Once the stage is empty of performers again voice recordings continue.*

MIC 3: [*voiceover*] 'I don't feel safe in here … I want to go to live somewhere better. Please kids in Australia, invite us to your country.'

A final round of microphones are placed on the stage by the performers.

The stage should now be full of microphones on stands. Once the stage is empty of performers again the final voice recording is played.

MIC 4: [*voiceover*] When I go to the soccer pitch, I look at the stars and I feel like I have power.

Slow lighting change as the audience is left to sit with this image for some time.

Blackout.

THE END

THE AUDITION

*Patricia Cornelius, Tes Lyssiotis, Sahra Davoudi,
Christos Tsiolkas, Melissa Reeves,
Milad Norouzi, Wahibe Moussa*

Peter Paltos and Sahra Davoudi in Outer Urban Projects' THE AUDITION (Photo: Darren Gill)

Introduction

The metaphor of the world as a theatre, or *theatrum mundi*, is an old one. 'All the world's a stage', writes Shakespeare, 'And all the men and women merely players' (*As You Like It*, Act II, Scene VII). However, not every player has equal access to the stage. Some—like royalty— are thrust into the spotlight by virtue of birth, race, gender, class and other privileges. Others are allowed to appear but are relegated to small parts, no matter how talented. Still others, like asylum seekers, are hidden off stage and subjected to endless auditions for the mere right to appear, let alone exercise agency.

This is the basic premise of *The Audition*—that the theatre is not only a metaphor for the world but a microcosm of it. Specifically, the theatre is a small-scale version of the nation-state, with borders, documents and protocols for passing. As the artistic director of Outer Urban Projects, Irine Vela, argues, 'a stage—like a country—has its own rules and regulations', and there are 'parallels in the processes experienced by actors seeking work and refugees seeking asylum'. In both cases, applicants wait while someone more powerful determines their future, often based on a single encounter. Those who are both actors and asylum seekers—as two of the cast were—find themselves doubly displaced in Australia, where stages are overwhelmingly white and migrant artists are often discriminated against.

The Audition is authored by four established playwrights (Patricia Cornelius, Tes Lyssiotis, Melissa Reeves and Christos Tsiolkas) and three emerging ones (Sahra Davoudi, Milad Norouzi and Wahibe Moussa). Vela, Cornelius, Reeves and Tsiolkas—along with Andrew Bovell—previously co-wrote two plays: *Who's Afraid of the Working Class?* (1998) and its companion piece, *Anthem* (2019). Staged 21 years apart, both plays tell four interweaving stories and feature characters who are alienated from mainstream Australia because they are, for example, migrants, women or working class. For her part, Lyssiotis wrote *Hotel Bonegilla* (1983), a play about a migrant camp that housed new arrivals from Europe between 1947 and 1971. For all four established writers, *The Audition* feels like a natural extension of their formal and political interests.

The three emerging playwrights may be less familiar to audiences, but they are no less central to the work. As Vela explains in her Director's Note, the play was 'inspired by two commanding young Iranian artists, Milad Norouzi and Sahra Davoudi, who were seeking asylum and permanent residency while developing and creating the work. As creators and performers, they imbue the show with a tension and truth that is palpable, poetic and at times absurd'. Wahibe Moussa's presence was not foregrounded in the publicity to the same extent, but she is one of several artists with migrant heritage. This is the link between the emerging and established playwrights as well as cast members. Without writing or speaking a word, these authors and actors performed an important act of inter-ethnic, inter-generational solidarity, linking the experiences of yesterday's migrants and refugees to those of today's asylum seekers.

The play opens with an electrifying monologue titled 'The Doll', written by Cornelius and performed by Mary Sitarenos. 'I come for Olive', she says, and at first, it is unclear whom she means. However, it becomes apparent that she is referring to Olive in Ray Lawler's iconic *Summer of the Seventeenth Doll* (1955). The character Olive lives in Melbourne and spends seven months of the year waiting for her sugarcane cutter boyfriend to reappear. The actor repeats Olive's name at least 12 times throughout the monologue, yet with each repetition, the possibility of her becoming Olive seems to recede. The actor believes she is 'a perfect Olive', but her agent says, 'Olive's Australian. Dinky-di Australian … Olive's a type … Olive's white'. One critic described this opening scene as 'a staggering histrionic display … a paean to the art of acting, a sensitive piece of theatre criticism that imagines Olive from the inside out, and slivers of the riveting performance our stages will be denied by implicitly racist casting' (Woodhead, 2019).

In another metatheatrical scene titled 'The Audition', authored by Tsiolkas, an Australian director ignores the lived experience and professional expertise of the actor he is auditioning to play Hecuba in *The Trojan Women*. The choice of play is no accident: directors have often turned to Ancient Greek tragedies for their depictions of hospitality and displacement (Wilmer 2018, 11). There is a famous production titled *Queens of Syria* (2013), where a cast of 15 Syrian refugee women played *The Trojan Women*. Here, the actor is originally from Iran, and has performed in Farsi and English—including Shakespeare in the original—and has colleagues across Europe. Regardless, the director's gendered and stereotyped vision prevails. These two actors then become an immigration official and an asylum seeker in Melissa Reeves' 'You made us a promise that what you told us today would be true', which depicts the refugee determination process, where gender and power once again reinforce each other. Similarly, the woman in Davoudi's piece 'Seven Days' recalls seven key moments in her migration and marriage, with each moment then coached and improved by her lawyer. The bride and the woman in Moussa's brief but forceful poem 'I Can Be Her' regard the process with an ironic, despairing distance.

While these scenes take place in rehearsal rooms and courtrooms, two others are set in detention. Lyssiotis's 'Woomera' depicts an immigration detention centre in 2001. The characters imprisoned within it turn their minds back to moments of departure, transit, arrival and now endless stasis. In Norouzi's poetic 'Beautiful Jail', which he also performs, the character laments the sky, clouds, stars, mountains, jungles and oceans he can see but cannot touch. The inability to touch pervades the entire play, which often feels profoundly anti-social, notwithstanding the interweaving stories and role doubling. In most scenes, characters are delivering monologues; occasionally, they are in dialogue but often speaking at cross purposes. The only scenes where more than two people appear are in 'Woomera', but the detainees are lost in their own lonely worlds. The overall effect is to convey the profound isolation produced by the detention system. It also suggests how individualised current solutions are when what is really needed is structural reform.

The Audition premiered at La Mama's Courthouse Theatre on 13 November 2019. La Mama has a tradition of holding a raffle every night, with 'everyone's tickets go[ing] into a draw for a prize that's usually linked to the show in some way—a jar of preserves, perhaps, or free tickets' (Croggon 2019). On opening night, the prize was a copy of the award-winning book *No Friend But the Mountains* by Behrouz Boochani, a Kurdish writer, filmmaker and journalist imprisoned on Manus for over six years. Incredibly, the night *The Audition* premiered was the night he was finally freed. Critics could not help but notice the coincidence, with one describing how surreal it was to check her Twitter feed on the way home and find that 'Boochani was free, taking part in a writers' festival in Christchurch, New Zealand' (Croggon 2019). Another proclaimed 'Behrouz Boochani is free because of a writers' festival in New Zealand. ... Telling stories is how creative minds find solutions to horror and work towards humanity. Telling stories ... is how Behrouz Boochani is finally FINALLY out of the hell that Australians put him in' (Peard 2019). Like *No Friend But the Mountains*, *The Audition* is an important document of this time; like the writers' festival, it gathered and galvanised an audience, reminding them that art might not do much, but sometimes it does far more than politics.

Tania Cañas and Caroline Wake

References

Croggon, Alison. 2019. 'The Audition'. *The Saturday Paper*, 23 November. https://www.thesaturdaypaper.com.au/2019/11/23/the-audition/15744276009120#hrd.

Peard, Anne-Marie. 2019. 'Not a Review: *The Audition*'. *Sometimes Melbourne*, 14 November. http://sometimesmelbourne.blogspot.com/2019/11/not-review-audition.html.

Wilmer, Steve. 2018. *Performing Statelessness in Europe*. Cham, Switzerland: Palgrave Macmillan.

Woodhead, Cameron. 2019. 'Political Theatre Doesn't Get Much Better Than This'. *The Age*, 15 November. https://www.theage.com.au/culture/theatre/political-theatre-doesn-t-get-much-better-than-this-20191115-p53ayh.html.

The Audition was first produced by Outer Urban Projects in partnership with La Mama at the Courthouse Theatre, Melbourne, on 14 November 2019, with the following cast:

PERFORMERS	Sahra Davoudi
	Mary Sitarenos
	Peter Paltos
	Milad Norouzi
	Vahideh Eisaei (musician)

Director, Dramaturg and Concept, Irine Vela
Co-Dramaturg, Maryanne Lynch
Lighting Designer, Gina Gascoigne
Costume and Set Designer, Adrienne Chisholm
Stage Manager, Genevieve Cizevskis

Writer *The Doll*, Patricia Cornelius
Writer *Woomera Detention Centre*, Tes Lyssiotis
Writer *Seven Days*, Sahra Davoudi
Writer *The Audition*, Christos Tsiolkas
Writer *You made us a promise what you told us today would be true*, Melissa Reeves
Writer *Beautiful Jail*, Milad Norouzi
Writer *I Can Be Her*, Wahibe Moussa

Kanun music and improvisations based on Iranian classical music modes, Vahideh Eisaei
Song 'Goodbye', Milad Norouzi
Musical Direction, Irine Vela

Outer Urban Projects Team

Artistic Director, Irine Vela
Executive Producer, Kate Gillick
General Manager, David Ralph
Finance Manager, Lani Hannah
Community Program Coordinator, Melanie Augustine
Cultural Community Development Worker, Akimera Burckhardt-Bedeau
Administration and Finance Officer, Peta Kalis
Marketing Assistant, Victoria Canning
Marketing Support Worker for *The Audition*, Vanessa Francesca
Audience Envoys for *The Audition*, Asha Beverage, Damian Seddon, Fakaoho Tupou, James Madsen-Smith, Katrina Deer
Publicity Consultant, Ben Starick, Starling Communications
Photographers (publications and rehearsals) Miguel Rios and Meredith O'Shea
Photographer (rehearsals), Sarah Walker
Photographer (rehearsals), Darren Gill
Videographer (dress), Meredith O'Shea

With special thanks to the La Mama team, Liz Jones, Caitlin Dullard, Sophia Constanine, Solange Parraguez, Hayley Fox, Amber Hart and Elena Larkin, Asylum Seeker Resource Centre team, Kon Karapanagiotidis and Nandini Bose, Brunswick Mechanics Institute team, Bobby Virgona and Magenta Sheridan, and the artists that were part of earlier creative developments: Ez Eldin Deng, Maryanne Sam, Tariro Mavondo, Marcus McKenzie, Marco Chiappi and Sapidah Kian.

Director's Note

In the ecology that Outer Urban Projects creates and inhabits, excellence in art is redefined as a form of protest and resistance—it is where ghettoised, ignored and compelling voices and bodies can aspire, thrive and inspire change because they have powerful stories to tell and the hunger and means to do so.

The Audition is inspired by two young Iranian artists Milad Norouzi and Sahra Davoudi who were seeking asylum and permanent residency while creating the work. Their situation imbued the creative process with a tension and truth that was palpable, poetic and at times absurd.

We then approached a diverse group of writers, emerging and established, to consider collaborating on a multi-authored theatre piece—we were emboldened by their excitement around the concept of the work and their delight in taking part in an Outer Urban Projects production

In developing the work we explored the experience of the audition process to understand the experience of seeking asylum and to gain insight into the protocols and power relationships that permit entry into our country and onto our stages.

The struggle to gain acceptance and recognise merit where and when it is due is always an ongoing tension. Theatre itself is political by virtue of who is represented on the stage and where the content comes from. So theatre itself is inherently political. The asylum seeker shares something in common with the actor in Australia. They are both outsiders of uncertain status.

Irine Vela, on behalf of Outer Urban Projects

CHARACTERS

The Doll
MARTA, actor in her 30s, second-generation immigrant

Woomera Detention Centre
MARYAM, Iranian refugee
SAHID, Afghani refugee, rug maker
NASRIN, Maryam's daughter, a young girl
MOHSEN, Maryam's husband

Seven Days
PARIYA, a woman in her early 20s from Iran
LAWYER

The Audition
AVA
VIDA
AUDITIONER

You made us a promise what you told us today would be true
MEMBER
APPLICANT 1
APPLICANT 2
APPLICANT 3

Beautiful Jail
A REHABILITATED INMATE

I Can Be Her
The ACTOR who plays Pariya

DOUBLING

MARTA, MARYAM, VIDA

SAHID, LAWYER, AUDITIONER, MEMBER

NASRIN, PARIYA, AVA, APPLICANT 1, ACTOR

APPLICANT 2, REHABILITATED INMATE

SETTING
A stage covered in sand. A makeshift swing. A soccer ball. A guitar. A plastic chair. A rug.

THE DOLL

MARTA *stands very still in the middle of the space. She looks out over the audience for some time.*

MARTA: I've got you. A little. Aroused your anticipation somewhat. It's in the gaze. Its intensity. I'll have you believe my eyes are the gateway to my soul. I see through you. I see beyond you. I see somewhere so far, so distant, somewhere utterly unfathomable, into the landscape of the existential, but of course I don't see anything at all.

I come for Olive.

' … compared to all the marriages I know, what I got is—[*groping with her depth of feeling*]—five months of heaven every year.'

I come to spill my guts, to reveal tender, raw, heart-rending stories. About myself. Not myself exactly. Because it's not me you see, of course it's not, but it is, of course it is. Who else can it be? It's me and it's not. Not my words but I own them, they're mine, I believe every word I say. As do you. I speak the truth.

Perhaps. If you don't believe me, demand your money back.

'**And it's the same for them—seven months they spend up there killin' themselves in the cane season, and then they come down here to live a little. That's what the lay-off is—not just playing around and spendin' a lot of money, but a time for livin'.**'

Words ride my breath, song-like, full of cadence, full of riffs and dips and cre-scen-dos. They trip along like a bubbling brook, dancing and prancing full of lovely highs and lows, clipped and running together like in an inexorably long list. I pause, allow the words to sit. Place—them—just—so. I raise my voice, authoritative, intimidating, in control. And louder, rude, obnoxious, ear-splitting. I stutter and splutter, let my voice drop low, almost inaudibly low. Bring you in close on a whisper. I tinge it with laughter, lovely, spluttering laughter, a big guffaw. Giggling's difficult but when it's successful it's a treat. As is the occasional shriek. I load it up, nice and heavy, full of gravitas, use its weight, deliver it like a slap to your face. A catch in my throat, a shift in my breath, like this, can bring you to tears. Blubbering like a child can work, but better, much, to suggest, bring to the brink of tears and delicately hold them back. The art of restraint.

It can make you ache.

The power in it, the magnificence of it, the playfulness, the joy, the skill, the gorgeous trickery.

I come for Olive. The quintessentially Australian Olive. I know her. Like the back of my hand. A woman on her own who lives for a dream that lasts five months each year. **'Five months of heaven,'** when the man she loves, Roo, a cane-cutter comes to her in the lay-off bearing yet another kewpie doll for her collection.

I know her well. The dream keeps her from the disappointments, from the loneliness of marriage with kids, from the lifelessness of the mundane. It's five months of laughter and romance, seeing a show, going to the races, drinking too much, having a ball. It's a heightened time and Olive lives for it.

'You think I haven't sized it up against what all those married women have? I laugh every time that they look down their noses at me. Even waiting for Roo to come back is more excitin' than their little lot … '

Olive's about wanting, about wanting more, about wanting to keep something precious, wanting life to be vital—at least for part of each year.

I adore Olive. Oh yes, I know her. She's from the Australian classic, *Summer of the Seventeenth Doll*, a play famous for the first to use the Australian vernacular, it's rhythms, it's sayings:

' … it's having another woman walking around knowing your inside and sorry for you 'coz she thinks you've never been within cooee of the real thing, that's what hurts.'

… says Olive.

This, the seventeenth year, things have changed and the dream shakes, it quivers, it fails to deliver. Olive takes us to the very edge—she teeters there.

'—I want what I had before. You give it back to me—give me back what you've taken.'

Silence.

But no, there's some mistake, an error made. My agent has got it wrong. There's no way I'm an Olive.

Oh but I am.

There's not a chance in hell you could play her.

I know her. I can.

You have an accent.

What accent? I'm Australian, I have an Australian accent.

Olive's Australian. Dinky di Australian.

As am I!

Olive's a type.

I can play it.

You don't look right.

I'm right, I'm a perfect Olive.

Olive's white.

MARTA *shakes her head. She quotes from Ray Lawler's play directions as she makes her departure:*

'OLIVE shakes her head dumbly. There is an unbelieving moment. She stumbles forward. Picks up her bag. It is the progress of a drunk woman. Wanders out of sight.'

WOOMERA DETENTION CENTRE

NASRIN *places a big stick on the ground, jumps playfully from one side to the other. At times her foot hovers between the two sides.*

NASRIN: Woomera, Australia. Woomera, Australia. Woomera, Australia.

SAHID: They watch me, all the time they watch me. Am I standing in the right position? Do I have the right posture? So, you freeze our applications? You say we destroyed your buildings in America. You tell me I am not Hazara that I don't look like one, and my accent is wrong. You say I am Tajik. You tell me I do not speak the truth but sometimes the truth is not easy to tell. I know what I'd like to say to you—I know this—you big, civilised countries talk democracy and human rights but you come to our country test your bombs and chemicals but you are not the loser. Maybe you fight ten, fifteen years, then you leave, but I can't speak your language, and you are *civilised*. I learn to follow your rules. I learn your words, yes means yes, no means no. You test me. Is this the punishment for surviving the boat? But I died many times, imprisonment, torture, interrogation, wars, each time the same just different bosses, swallowed by the ocean but I came back. Or am I dead already? I am afraid of forgetting.

After many months of detention, MOHSEN *has lost hope. He lies inert under a blanket, by his wife's side.*

MARYAM: Mohsen, oh that's alright. You can just lie there. Hide. No-one is talking. You don't talk, your daughter doesn't talk. The man doesn't talk to us. You can't speak to these people. They are too busy building fences in case we escape into the desert. Remember what we said? A new start, no trouble? And yet, there you were, involved in the riots. I suppose you took your camera with you, maybe that's why they haven't given us the visa. Why must you speak your mind? Evin Prison wasn't enough? I waited seven years for you. Don't you forget that. We can't fail now.

She nudges him.

BEAUTIFUL JAIL

REHABILITATED INMATE: Is there such thing as heaven or hell? I sense the answer but I'm not sure if I'm right or wrong. After five spring time, I can't remember maybe six or seven, I haven't seen my parents and they are terribly sick and they are talking about their time to die coming closer. We are running out of time. I feel I may never see them again without knowing what they wanted for me. This is when I realise I'm in seven thousand, six hundred and ninety-two million kilometre squared beautiful jail called Australia.

SEVEN DAYS

PARIYA: I knew Australia is a big country but I had no idea it's this big. It took us such a long time from Darwin to Melbourne. I was looking at the map on plane's monitor and I was wondering why isn't this journey finishing?

I can see the lights. I'm in Melbourne.

My destination. Where I'm gonna find love and happiness. I'll be a bride soon. I hope I can find a bathroom and mirror before he sees me. I need to be beautiful.

Why people in this queue are all anxious and nervous? Two Asian girl are looking for something in their backpack. Oh, what about those two pack of saffron with me? Okay, I have everything that I need, my password, the printed visa just in case, the form they gave me in the plane and … why even my mum insist on having saffron? I don't know how to cook. But it's the tradition you know. Saffron is given to everyone who goes from Iran, like this is the only thing you might wish for in another country, like everything else is fine and you are going to sit in your luxury villa while looking at sunset and having your wine and caviar, you will just sigh heavily, ahhhhhh … if only … I had a pack of saffron.

There he is. I can see him. I can see he just had a shave and haircut. I can see in his eyes he didn't sleep much last night. He can't even remember where he parked his car. But nothing is important. We are walking hand in hand in airport car park looking for his missing car.

Oh my god. Look at this place, no blurring horns, no busy streets, no high rise, just houses with gable roofs and gardens next to each other. No traffic? This just looks like northern Iran. I wanna live in one of these houses. I love it.

AVA AND VIDA

AVA *is before a mirror, getting ready for her audition. Her friend,* VIDA, *is looking over her shoulder.*

VIDA: Too much make-up.
AVA: You think?
VIDA: Yes. Take it easy with the eye shadow.
AVA: It doesn't matter what she's suffered and what she's lost. She will make herself up, she will not show her age, she will refuse to act like the slave she now is.

When the audience first sees her she must be beautiful. They must know that she is still a queen.

VIDA: You're thinking like a Persian. You've got to think like an Australian woman.

AVA: The character isn't Australian.

VIDA: But the production is Australian. Trust me, they'll think you look slutty.

AVA: [*almost as if in prayer*] I really want this part. I really need this part. [*Turning to* VIDA] Is this dress okay?

VIDA: It's fine. But wear black tights with it. Don't show bare leg. And don't wear high heels. Wear your black flats.

AVA: But they make me look short.

VIDA: You are short.

AVA: That's why I thought the high heels …

VIDA: [*interrupting*] Elegant but sturdy shoes. That's what you should wear. You'll have a better chance if they think you're a feminist.

AVA: I am a feminist.

VIDA: Their kind of feminist.

AVA: [*starts reciting a few lines from Euripides'* The Trojan Women] Such grief!

How can I not groan with pain when I have lost it all? Everything. I've lost my country, my children, my husband!

VIDA: Too stern. Be more emotional.

AVA: That's not how to play her. She's lost everything: she says that! The one thing they can't take from her is her dignity.

VIDA: I think you need to be more emotional.

AVA: [*deliberately melodramatic*] Such grief!

How can I not groan with pain when I have lost it all? Everything. I've lost my country, my children, my husband! I'm a helpless little refugee. Help me help me.

Silence.

Better?

VIDA: I've been here longer.

I know the games you have to play. To make them let you stay. To make them let you work. To make them think they're doing you a favour.

Do you want this part?

AVA: Of course I do.

VIDA: Then play it as if she's begging. And have a sad smile right at the end. They'll love that.
AVA: This character would not smile. I know her. She would not smile.
VIDA: They'll think you're hard.
AVA: She ruled a world. And it was stolen from her. I will not smile.
VIDA: Okay, okay. Don't smile during the scene. But straight afterwards, give them a half-smile, be a little girlish, say something like, 'Was that alright?'
AVA: Now that sounds sluttish.
VIDA: No. Deference is good. It's sexual confidence you can't show.
AVA: They don't have it, do they?
VIDA: What don't they have?
AVA: That. They don't have any sexual confidence. They think they do or they try and pretend they do. But it's all masks and costumes.
VIDA: Yes, they're terrified of sex.
AVA: Are we being harsh?
VIDA: They don't need compassion.
> They're children. Their culture, their history, their ... their ... their ... their spirit is that of a child. They're soft and cruel all at the same time.
> They're just fucking spoiled children.
> Play her as a child. Maybe they'll give you the part then.

AVA: She is not a child. What she has seen has torn all her innocence from her. How could I play this woman as a child?
VIDA: Do you want the part?
AVA: You know I do.
> I'm desperate to work.

VIDA: Then play her as a child. Be a child, a hurt sad traumatised little infant.
> It's not a guarantee but if you want the part, that's how you should play her.

> *AVA gets up from the mirror. She faces the audience.*
>
> *She starts reciting the lines from the play, her voice that of a distressed young woman.*

AVA: Such grief!
> How can I ... [*Breaking out of character*] NO,
> I will not play her like that. That is to betray her.

VIDA: Then you're fucked.

YOU MADE US A PROMISE WHAT YOU TOLD US TODAY WOULD BE TRUE

MEMBER: Applicant One, you're clear about what's happening today?
APPLICANT 1: Yes.
MEMBER: You understand that this is the last time you can ask for protection. There are no more appeals after this.

> APPLICANT 1 *nods*.

You have no more papers to give me? You have given me all the documents that you have prepared?

> APPLICANT 1 *nods*.

I understand your marriage wasn't happy?
APPLICANT 1: No, it wasn't.
MEMBER: Can you tell me more about the reason your marriage broke down?
APPLICANT 1: I stopped going to mosque and I started going to services at the Glenroy Baptist Mission Church.
MEMBER: I set a bit of store by my first look at the applicant. I've read their file, and I've got a pretty good idea about what I think of their case. The first eye contact can change things completely.
APPLICANT 1: If I return to Iraq, I will be tortured or made to reconvert or killed by extremist Muslims or any Muslims because now I'm a Christian.
MEMBER: This letter, from the rector of the Baptist Church, Margaret Perkin, confirms that you have been attending her church since the beginning of 2018. Is that correct?
APPLICANT 1: Yes.
MEMBER: But this date is six months after your marriage ended. Do you have an explanation for that?
APPLICANT 1: Yes, no I went before, not official, but I went.
MEMBER: So, this date is wrong?
APPLICANT 1: Yes, I went before.
MEMBER: Your husband claims that you were the one to leave the marriage, that you had moved away from him and were living in Perth with another man. Is this true?

APPLICANT 1: No. That is not true. He is lying because he doesn't want anything good to happen to me.

MEMBER: If you get a certain sort of member, the sort of member who wants to see you succeed, they might overlook those tiny tell-tale signs, they'll give you the benefit of the doubt, but if you get another sort of member, one who's been parachuted in from a totally unrelated department, transferred, say, from employment and infrastructure, if they get the slightest whiff of deception, or even if they just don't take to you particularly, they'll affirm the decision to refuse a protection visa in a trice. Have you been to Perth?

APPLICANT 1: Yes, but that is because I have relatives there.

MEMBER: I'm in the middle of those two sorts of members.

APPLICANT 1: It's my husband. It's him who is not been faithful.

MEMBER: I've booked in for massage at a place in the city centre. It's in my lunch hour and I'll have to belt over there, but it'll be worth it. I ache. Up my spine, and round underneath my jaw, a dull persistent ache, around my mouth and my cheeks, across the bridge of my nose, especially around my eyes. My face feels like it's been cast in plaster of Paris and left to dry. I think I have fibromyalgia.

APPLICANT 1: The Baptist Church was very close to our apartment, and I started going there as a quiet place to sit, then I got talking to the rector, Margaret Perkin, she was very sympathetic. I told her my story and I decided to become a Christian.

Pause.

I'm tired of all the trouble that comes with the Muslim religion, the conflict between Sunnis and Shias in my country.

Pause, starts to cry.

I'm very depressed, I'm on medication.

MEMBER: I feel sorry for her.

APPLICANT 1: My childhood was full of fear. I have felt sad my whole life.

MEMBER *passes her a tissue.*

MEMBER: But the sad fact is that we're not here to make judgments on the basis of sympathy. People melt your heart. Their persistence, their endless attempts to better their situation, their soul, like the young man I saw last week.

A young man, APPLICANT 2 *appears, facing the audience.*

A chef who wanted more time. This was a multiple hearing, eight identical cases, all with the same immoveable legal sticking point, and one by one, after listening to their story, I told them, very gently, that there will be no more time, we will process their cases very fast, we have been criticised for being slow in the past, and now we are quick, and they would get their determinations by the end of June, and they would be decisions to affirm, and they will have twenty-eight days to arrange their departure from Australia. This young man had been working for the Traralgon Golf Club.

APPLICANT 2: I was sponsored for a four-five-seven visa.

MEMBER: But when the whether got cold, they let him go. The manager, Ron Latham, withdrew their sponsorship, and even though that's very unfair—

APPLICANT 2: I begged him.

MEMBER: —and it's not the young man's fault—

APPLICANT 2: I said Ron please, don't play with my future.

MEMBER: —there can be only one result, whether he finds another job, or gets another sponsor, it is only the first sponsor and the first application that matters. This young man did get another job, at a bakery in Richmond, and when that fell through, he got another, in a café in Port Melbourne. I liked his pluck.

APPLICANT 2: I'm a qualified and talented chef. If I can keep working until August, it will be three years and I can apply for permanent residency.

MEMBER: I had left this man till last.

APPLICANT 2: I just need time.

MEMBER: He has sad eyes and a soft determined voice. He had tried so hard, this young man, like the others, they had all tried hard, but he had tried even harder, and he deserved a break, I thought.

MEMBER *and* APPLICANT 2 *gaze at each other.*

What date in August do you have to work to?

APPLICANT 2: Sir, I have to work to eighteenth of August.

MEMBER: I can't guarantee that your determination will not come till then, but sometimes these things take time …

And he knew and I knew that I would delay his case, of all the cases I heard that day, his would be the one that shifted me.

MEMBER *shifts his gaze back to* APPLICANT 1.

What was your husband studying here in Australia?

APPLICANT 1: I'm not sure.

MEMBER: You don't know what your husband was studying?

APPLICANT 1: Something in business.

MEMBER: Business studies?

APPLICANT 1: Not business studies, no.

MEMBER: If you had to hazard a guess, what would you say?

APPLICANT 1: I think it was to do with property development.

MEMBER: There is always a tiny flame of fear that ignites when you reject their appeal and send them back.

Once I affirmed a decision to reject a protection visa for a young Egyptian woman. She had a flimsy case. There was no way round it. She engaged a lawyer to help her, at great expense, but nothing was going to help her case. She had waited for a long time and become very depressed.

MEMBER *and* APPLICANT 3 *gaze at each other for few seconds.*

She jumped from the balcony of her high-rise building the day she received her determination.

MEMBER *returns his gaze to* APPLICANT 1.

Did your husband earn a qualification or degree?

APPLICANT 1: I'm not sure. I don't think so.

MEMBER: This job has soured the world for me. I don't read books. Or watch much television. I have found myself a hobby. Embroidery. I listen to chamber music and I embroider. When I started I would stick closely to the pattern, but now I'm much more free-hand. I put little surprises in my designs. Small visual jokes. I hide a snail in amongst flowers, or I put a greedy little mouse next to cheese and biscuits. My last piece was a table cloth with a Spanish theme. Bulls, bull-fighters, castanets, flamenco dancers, and in the middle I embroidered a enormous pan of paella, with all the elements individually rendered, mussels, red pepper, rice, chorizo, green beans, and lovely pure white circles of calamari.

Moves to APPLICANT 1.

Is there anything else you can tell me to help me to understand why it is dangerous for you to return to Iraq?

APPLICANT 1 *looks at the audience. Pause.*

All rise.

WOOMERA DETENTION CENTRE

MARYAM: [*addressing her husband once again*] Ask the man again, maybe you didn't speak to him properly or maybe you missed some points in the interview, or maybe I made a mistake. The interpreter was hard to understand. Are you listening Mohsen? Speak to me.

BEAUTIFUL JAIL

A REHABILITATED INMATE: The sky is soft. I have never touched it but I can feel it is. Sometimes I wish I was or is it better to say I wish I could turn into a bird then I could fly far far away from this beautiful jail. The cool breeze is nice when you fly with it. The sun is so generous even though we are living far away from it.

The clouds are fluffy and sweet.

God turn me into a bird then I could fly far far away from this beautiful jail. The stars look friendly. I want to talk to them.

I need to tell them my secrets.

The moon is white, as white as a pure spirit. The mountains are full of joy.

The jungle is full of surprises. The Milky Way is full of secrets.

God turn me into a bird then I could fly far far away from this beautiful jail. I'm begging you god, hear me only once.

Everyone here walked away from me,

Everyone forced me to accept their opinions, did you? My life is too short, as short as my blue pen's life.

God turn me into a bird then I could fly far far away from this beautiful jail. The female deer doesn't take care of her fawn.

Poor people are dying day after day. Time flies. Life passes quickly.

Babies are born, babies are toddlers, toddlers are kids, kids are teenagers, teenagers are adults, adults are middle ages, middle ages are old people, they are dying.

God turn me into a bird then I could fly far far away from this beautiful jail.

I dreamed. I dreamed of the migrating birds, I was flying with them. We were heading north. No borders, no boundaries, it was just us, flying freely.

AVA AND VIDA

AVA *is sitting on stage. The* AUDITIONER *is standing, his back to the audience.*

AVA: [*distraught, almost meek*] Such grief!
How can I not groan with …

> AVA *stops. Looks up.*

Sorry. Can I try it once more?
AUDITIONER: [*stands up*] Yes. Take your time.

> AVA *stands up. She repeats the scene but this time with an unsentimental, almost grim delivery.*

AVA: Such grief!
How can I not groan with pain when I have lost it all?
Everything. I've lost my country, my children, my husband! For generations, mountains of glorious wealth passed down to us and now all of it has vanished. Now it is nothing, all of it is gone.

Now, will I no longer be allowed to speak my tongue? What language will I be forced to use?

What should I mourn? How should I mourn? How unbearable is my fate!

> AVA *looks up expectantly.*

AUDITIONER: Thank you Ava.
I understand what you're trying to do, and it's good. I like that she remains regal. But the danger in that choice is that it might be too restrained.

Hecuba is devastated. Her world has gone. Her family is lost. We need to feel that.

AVA: I know this woman. All that remains to her is dignity. I wanted to play that. She won't beg. If she begs all is lost to her.

AUDITIONER: Isn't the tragedy that dignity too is stripped from her in the end? This play is about total devastation, it is about what war does to women …

AVA: [*interrupting*] … I know this play. I have performed this part before.

AUDITIONER: When?

AVA: In Tehran.

AUDITIONER: I wouldn't have thought The Trojan Women would have been popular with … with your regime?

AVA: Euripides has been performed in Farsi for a long time.

AUDITIONER: Your CV is very impressive. Tantalising, really, the range of your work. But you haven't worked in the theatre here, have you?

AVA: No.

AUDITIONER: So you've never performed in English?

AVA: I have.

I worked with a great director in Tehran. She had us perform *The Tempest* in the original English.

AUDITIONER: Why?

AVA: To understand the language, and then go beyond the language. That's how she explained it to us. I didn't understand it at first but working on the play it began to make sense.

Everything I know about the English language I learnt from that production.

AUDITIONER: What did you learn?

AVA: That English is a young language. That it's playful and that's where its beauty lies. It's a trickster's language.

AUDITIONER: I'm not sure I understand?

AVA: Words have double or triple meanings.

AUDITIONER: You were Miranda?

AVA: I played Ariel.

AUDITIONER: Well, yes, she is a trickster.

AVA: That isn't what I meant.

AUDITIONER: Then what did you mean?

AVA: To enjoy the … [*In Farsi: How do I explain this? 'chejoori begam?'*] play of the language, I must not be … not scared … I must not be …

AUDITIONER: Intimidated?

AVA: Yes! That is correct. I must not be intimidated by the language.
AUDITIONER: And the director? Of that production? Is she still working in …
AVA: [*interrupting*] … She's in Sweden. Last I heard she's in Gothenburg.
AUDITIONER: Working in theatre there?
AVA: No.
AUDITIONER: I am sorry.
AVA: For what?
AUDITIONER: For …

> AVA *and the* AUDITIONER *stare at each other.*

I believe you when you say you know this character.
My original intention had been to have everyone in this production speak in broad Aussie accents …
AVA: … I can work on my accent.
AUDITIONER: [*holding up his hand*] Hold on, hold on. Let me finish.
I want this fucked-up country to understand what it is to be a refugee, to be exiled, to lose everything. To try and get this fucked-up racist country to walk in another's shoes for once. To make Australians think: what would I do if this calamity happened to me?
That's what I want from this production.

> *Silence.*

Do you understand me?
AVA: That's true for every production of *The Trojan Women*.
AUDITIONER: Then we received your CV and I became curious about what we could gain by having an actual refugee in the role.
AVA: I know this woman. As an actor I know her.
AUDITIONER: I'd like you to do that scene again.
AVA: Of course.
AUDITIONER: And don't worry about the accent. I was wrong. Use your accent, that's who we are.

> AVA *stands in front of audience. She is about to begin her audition once more.*

Before you start … let's … let's use this scarf as a hijab!
AVA: Why?

AUDITIONER: I'd like to try it.
AVA: What?
AUDITIONER: If you don't want to do it then you don't have to.

 I just think that having the women wear the hijab might make the connections I wish to draw between the Trojan War and our contemporary world a little clearer.

 But I don't want you to do anything that makes you uncomfortable.

Silence.

AVA: I can do it.
AUDITIONER: That's great.

> AVA *wears the hijab loose. The* AUDITIONER *guides her to wear it tighter.*

That's absolutely great.

 And I want you here. Right up front.

> AVA *walks to the front of the stage.*

Further in, A bit ... I want you in the sand.
AVA: [*steps in the sand*] Such grief!
AUDITIONER: [*interrupting*] Everything she had has been lost. I want to feel it.
AVA: [*with severity, almost coldly*] Such grief!

 How can I not groan with pain when I have lost it all? Everything. I've lost my country, my children, my husband!
AUDITIONER: I want to see her really suffering!

> *The light is on* AVA. *She is attempting to smile. It comes slowly, as if she is struggling to align her face to the gesture of a smile. The smile is almost hideous in how forced it is. It is as much a howl as it is a smile.*
>
> *The stage goes black.*

SEVEN DAYS

LAWYER: What is your full name?
PARIYA: Pariya Miri
LAWYER: Why did you come to Australia?
PARIYA: I came here to get married.

LAWYER: But you didn't get married?
PARIYA: My ex-fiancé left me and now my visa has cancelled.
LAWYER: Why can't you go back to your country?
PARIYA: I can't go back, if I go I only have seven days before I die.
LAWYER: You will die. Good. That language will help the case. How will this happen?
PARIYA: On first day back in Iran, my family will come to the airport. they will wipe their tears, they will hug me tight, they will say 'it's alright. It's gonna be alright'.
LAWYER: This means failure. You were engaged to this man. He left you. You were neshoon karde.
PARIYA: On second day my friends will come to cheer me up. They will say 'he didn't deserve you, oh sweety, don't get upset, don't feel down.' It means I suppose to feel down and upset.
LAWYER: And what will you do?
PARIYA: On third day, no-one will come to cheer me up anymore. Good. The beginning of my normal life. I should get up and start over. I'll go sign up to a gym, look for a job. On fourth day, I'll meet a new person. Someone who doesn't know about my past. We are gonna hang out. We are gonna get to know each other more. He is a friend, he won't judge me. I'll tell him about my past. He is funny, I kinda like him.
LAWYER: Fifth day Pariya, what will happen on the fifth day?
PARIYA: The boy sympathises with me at first but then he changes. He starts to gossip about me, I won't tell the truth anymore. I won't tell the truth to the new people in my life anymore. I lie to them. I feel guilty. I become two person—one with a mask and one without. On sixth day, I'll stay inside. I throw out the mask. I'm drowning.
LAWYER: Seventh day, Pariya? What will happen?
PARIYA: I won't have a voice anymore. That's my case.
LAWYER: Your case is weak. It's not enough. Won't work.
PARIYA: What should I do?
LAWYER: Let's try again. What is your full name?
PARIYA: Pariya Miri.
LAWYER: Why did you come to Australia?
PARIYA: I came here to get married.
LAWYER: But you didn't get married.

PARIYA: I didn't get married because I didn't get along with my ex-fiancé.
LAWYER: Paria! Please answer every question carefully. This will help you to stay in the country. So why didn't you get married? Was your ex-fiancé violent towards you?
PARIYA: What do you mean by violence?
LAWYER: Hitting you? Imprisoning you? Raping you?

Now, you are a social outcast. A fallen woman. So why can't you return to your country?
PARIYA: Because they will kill me.

    PARIYA *comes to the front of stage:*

I CAN BE HER

LAILA *is an actor, auditioning for a TV show. She speaks in an accented English. She is passionate but can be playful and has learnt to channel her anger into humour.*

LAILA *is being recorded and her image is projected onto a screen for the audience.*

Alternately, LAILA *could address the audience directly as though looking into a camera.*

Enter LAILA *as herself.*

LAILA: My name is Laila Alizadeh, for Saleema, in *City Streets*.

    There is a moment as the actor prepares.

What do you want me to be?
  Who do you want to see?
  I can be her

  Listen
  I've been a
  Teacher and a poet
  A lover
  A hooker
  I can be a Kung Fu ninja
  A cop baiting traps for a killer
  Maybe a scientist
    Out to save the planet!

THE AUDITION

> I can lose my accent
> Give me a chance!

Begins to put on a hijab (covering her head and neck, not her face). Her movements are stylised, almost choreographed, at times she almost dances with the scarf.

Listen

> I've played the victim before
> I'm over this frightened
> loser you adore
> She makes me feel like a whore
> Saleema the Good
>   the suffering
>   the stuttering
>
> Under her scarf I'm naked
> Searching for her humanity
> My tongue is crippled
> In your language
> [*As Saleema*] Save me!
> This isn't the dream
> I fought for
> Plotted and risked my life for
> I've tasted blood on my name
> For mine and my sisters' freedom
>
> *If I do it your way just this once more*
> *Maybe you'll open the door*
>
> Only, every time I play this part
> It kills a piece of hope in me
> As though I agree
> To forget my whole identity
>
> But if I do it your way just this once more ...

> LAILA *stands wearing the hijab, looking into the camera.*

VOICEOVER: Thanks Laila. Good luck.

WOOMERA DETENTION CENTRE

NASRIN *paces around the perimeter of the compound, counting her steps.*

NASRIN: One, two, three, four, five … five hundred and forty-five days in India compound. And for seven days Baba is not eating. They now say every Iranian is being rejected.
Where are we?
It's the old house. Madar bozorg's and Pedar bozorg's. We are under the persimmon tree. It's autumn and the tree is full.

NASRIN *uses the big stick to draw images of each family member in the red dirt.*

This is my aunt Neda with worried eyes and big frown, they all frown in Maman's family. And they just argued over a recipe:
'—mage nagofti darchin beriz?
—goftam choobesho bendaz.'
Sara, Nasim, funny Aunt Esta, before she went into hiding, but no-one in the family is talking about it. Donya, my favorite aunt, with long long long dark hair just like Scheherazade, she speaks French and English and she studied in England. I wanna go there too. Why couldn't the people smugglers, have taken me there? Ahmad and Bahram, my brothers, they are talking to Uncle Omid from America and asking him about Bruce Lee for the third time. This is Baba, with happy face, and this is Maman frowning at Uncle Omid. And me, Nasrin. My name is Nasrin. It means a wild rose. [*Looking at camera in the camp*] My name is Nasrin. Nasrin.

Song.

A REHABILITATED INMATE:
>Goodbye
>To the sun, to the moon
>Goodbye, to the stars, to the sky
>Goodbye, to the oceans, to the sea
>Goodbye, wipe you tears from off your cheeks.

Music.

SAHID: What colour were her eyes? I want to remember. I can still see the ocean, shimmering out there, Meena's billowing skirt fanning the dark waters. What colour were her eyes? We don't have the technology of China and India but a good rug is made from the heart. And the finest quality wool, comes from Afghanistan. Remember our lessons Meena? I know you do. You would close your eyes and pretend to be asleep but I know you were listening. What colour eyes? Double weave, hear the shrieks, blue and deep, all the dead voices, drowned dreams, suffocated in brine and gasoline, too many, we were too many, my God. We were too many. Brown eyes? The weave must be tight, tight to be a true Afghan rug, a furious monster, deep, red, a relentless sea beast swooped on us, devouring us and sucked you out of my arms into deep, deep blue, your yellow head scarf drifted by and me clinging to the body of a dead woman. Feel the surface carefully with your palm. Smell, touch. There is no shininess just natural dyes.

We do not use chemicals, pitch black, her long, curly black hair threading the waves, deep blue and black, double weave our border all along the length, white helicopters and brown tanks. You can not rush the making of a fine rug Meena, it can take a year or more but I am a patient man. And I want to remember what are the colour of my daughter's eyes?

Sings his song:

A REHABILITATED INMATE:
    This is the last song I've written for you
    I haven't got much time to live I believe
    In this peace there are no blossoms on the trees
    The sky is cloudy but no rain is falling
    Goodbye
    To the sun, to the moon
    Goodbye, to the stars, to the sky
    Goodbye, to the oceans, to the sea
    Goodbye, wipe you tears from off your cheeks.

NASRIN: I'm the only girl left in here from my boat.

THE END

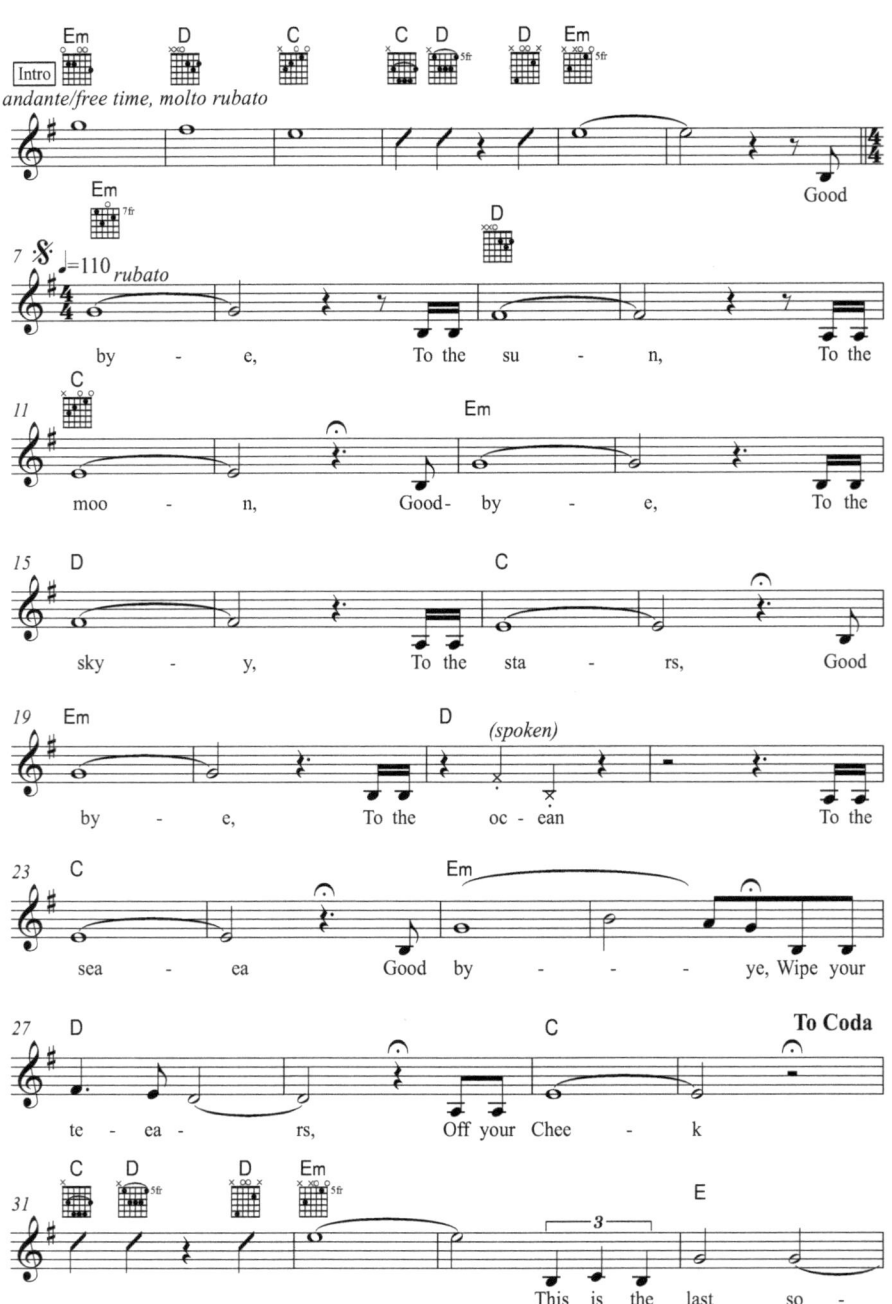

RELATED TITLES FROM CURRENCY PRESS

Staging Asylum
edited by Emma Cox

'While the theatre stands up for the despised, Australian culture and decency are not yet dead.' — Thomas Keneally

The first of its kind, this timely anthology brings together six contemporary Australian plays that offer a range of narratives and perspectives on asylum seekers. A vexed issue within the Australian community—particularly among politicians, who often use asylum seekers to further their own ends—this collection contributes to Australia's ongoing discourse on unauthorised asylum seekers, immigration detention, border control and the right to belong.

This eclectic collection includes *CMI (A Certain Maritime Incident)* by version 1.0, a smart, ironic verbatim work that deals with the Children Overboard Affair and the SIEV X disaster; *The Rainbow Dark* by Victoria Carless, a surreal domestic satire about immigration detention; *The Pacific Solution* by Ben Eltham, which takes armchair cricket commentary as a point of departure for a farce about the Howard government's excision of migration territory; *Halal-el-Mashakel* by Linda Jaivin, which looks at the friendship between two detained asylum seekers; *Journey of Asylum – Waiting* devised by Catherine Simmonds, a series of vignettes based upon the personal experiences of asylum seekers and refugees living in Melbourne; and *Nothing But Nothing* by Towfiq Al-Qady, an autobiographical play about childhood and war.

With a main Introduction as well as separate introductions to each play by editor and drama lecturer Dr Emma Cox, *Staging Asylum* recognises the crucial role that theatre has played—and continues to play—in one of Australia's most hotly debated and urgent contemporary issues.

9780868199832, also available as a digital edition.

FOR MORE PLAYS FROM WRITERS FEATURED IN THIS COLLECTION,
SEE OUR WEBSITE:
WWW.CURRENCY.COM.AU

www.currency.com.au

Visit Currency Press' website now to:
- Buy your books online
- Browse through our full list of titles, from plays to screenplays, books on theatre, film and music, and more
- Choose a play for your school or amateur performance group by cast size and gender
- Obtain information about performance rights
- Find out about theatre productions and other performing arts news across Australia
- For students, read our study guides
- For teachers, access syllabus and other relevant information
- Sign up for our email newsletter

The performing arts publisher

www.ingramcontent.com/pod-product-compliance
Lightning Source LLC
Chambersburg PA
CBHW040306170426
43194CB00022B/2922